THE CITY OF
BATH

Frontispiece. The Circus (in the foreground) and Royal crescent from the air, looking to the west.

THE CITY OF
BATH

BARRY CUNLIFFE

Yale University Press
New Haven and London

First published in Great Britain in 1986 by Alan Sutton Publishing
Published in the United States in 1987 by Yale University Press

Library of Congress catalog card number: 86–50624

International standard book number: 0–300–03808–9

Designed by Richard Bryant
Cover Design by Martin Latham
Typesetting and origination by
Alan Sutton Publishing Limited
Printed in Great Britain

CONTENTS

Picture Credits

The illustrations for this book have been collected from a variety of sources. Most of the line drawings were prepared by the author and sources have been given in the captions with additonal credits when necessary. Chris Unwin helped in the final preparation of much of this material. All photographs of maps and prints and the views of contemporary buildings were taken by Bob Wilkins and Paolo Scremin of the Institute of Archaeology at Oxford. We are most grateful to Stephen Bird, Curator of the Roman Baths Museum for his help in researching the original material in the Bath reference library, the City Archives and the Bath Art Gallery, and to the officials of those institutions for making their collections available to us.

Additional material was provided by Fotek Ltd., Bath (Frontispiece, ills. 5 and 10), Bath Museums Service (ills. 19, 30, 128, 129), David Burnett of The Dovecote Press Ltd. (ills. 117, 126, 132), Wessex Newspapers (ill. 133), Sir John Soane's Museum (ills. 103, 106), The British Museum (ills. 34, 72), The Cathedral Library, Exeter (ill. 38), Peter Davenport of the Bath Archaeological Trust (ill. 54).

PREFACE

THIS BOOK is a pure self-indulgence. Pretending to be at work I have allowed myself the exquisite luxury of spending autumn evenings writing about the city I love. Our relationship has been long-lived. For thirty years my professional involvement with Bath has caused me to learn her subtleties and with the learning has come an ever deepening appreciation. Walking about the streets there is a comforting familiarity that comes of long association – the sudden rise in street level at the end of Union Passage is caused by the rampart and ancient rubbish heaped up behind the city wall, the little alley opening from the east side of Broad Street just north of Bridge Street is the medieval Alford Lane which once led down to a ford across the Avon, long preceding Pulteney Bridge, and probably Roman or even earlier in origin, and that scrap of rough stone walling at the north end of the Marks and Spencers alley is the only surviving part of the abbey precinct wall built by the Bishop John of Tours in the late eleventh century when he acquired the burnt out ruins of the city from the king. All scraps of inconsequence perhaps – but together they are the city as much as its justly famous Roman baths and Georgian terraces.

The theme which we set out to explore here is a simple one – it is that the landscape influences man's actions and the actions of one generation constrict those of the next. In terms of the story of Bath hot springs and natural river crossings attracted man but once there and settled, boundaries were created: the wall put up by the Romans continued to be used in Saxon and medieval times as a defence and though now irrelevant and largely gone its ghost is still present in the street pattern and the building lines – causing constant traffic problems. It is very rarely that one generation sweeps away the boundaries of its predecessors – rather they are preserved like scar-tissue embedded in the city's growth.

The perspective of an historian, and the even deeper perspective of an archaeologist, often helps to put the more recent events into balance. The now-almost unbelievable destruction of the 1960s and early 70s caused, quite rightly, an anguished outcry from people who loved Bath, but was it any worse than John of Tours' total replanning of the south-eastern quarter of the old Saxon town, or the thrusting of brash new terraces into Bath's green belt in the eighteenth century? All these were acts of irreversible change and as such all will have had their critics. A city, after all, is only a fossilization of man's achievements and mistakes; all we can do is to attempt, by strength of public feeling, to constrain the scope for error.

This book, then, is an attempt to tell the story of a city, warts and all, and to show how the city we now enjoy came about. If it encourages the reader to stop, to think, to look about and to want to know more, it will have served its purpose.

Barry Cunliffe
Oxford
New Year's Eve 1985

1. LANDSCAPE AND MAN

THE SOUTHERN END of the Cotswolds is dramatic. It is a sudden, almost grandiose, landscape of flat-topped hills separated one from another by deeply incised river valleys cutting down through thick horizontally-bedded oolitic limestone into the softer Jurassic rocks beneath. The largest of the rivers is the Avon, snaking from east to west across the limestone uplands in a wide flat-bottomed valley fringed in places by gravel terraces and almost choked with its own alluvium (ill. 1). In prehistoric times it would have served as a line of communication from the Bristol Channel eastwards into the heartland of Wessex and to the Thames valley. Another route of equal importance was the Jurassic Way leading, along the Cotswolds, across Britain from the east coast to the shores of Dorset. The track chose to cross the Avon where the slopes were gentle and the valley flanks were firm and it was here that Bath had its beginnings.

The site of Bath is a low, wide ridge of blue Lias clay rising above the floor of the valley and surrounded on three sides by the meandering river. It is like being in the centre of a vast arena dominated by the cliff-like limestone hills which seem to surround it. From the hills themselves, looking down, Bath is the visual focus. It is also a focus of wonder for here, in the centre of the clay ridge, more than a quarter of a million gallons of hot mineral water gush out of the ground every day.

There are three hot springs in Bath, the King's Bath spring, the Hot Bath (or Hetling) spring and the Cross Bath spring. All were in existence in the Roman period and all were probably of very ancient origin. Recent excavations around the King's Bath spring have produced flint implements and debris dating from the Mesolithic period *c.* 5000 BC – a reminder of how alluring these hot springs would have been to the bands of early food gatherers who inhabited south-western Britain. The springs provided comfortable places to camp but they were also attractive to birds and wild animals which could have been captured hereabouts with comparative ease.

To understand the origins of the hot water we must make a brief excursion into the geological structure of north Somerset. Deep beneath the more recent rocks of the Triassic and Jurassic periods lie the much older rocks of Carboniferous and Devonian times (ill. 2). These older strata are not horizontally bedded but are depressed in the centre forming a deep bowl, the south lip of which outcrops now as the Mendips. The north-eastern lip comes close to the surface near Bath, but is buried beneath more recent deposits while the western edge outcrops

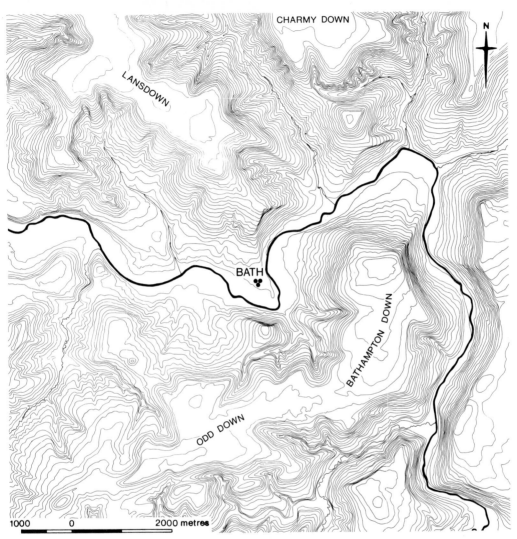

1.   The prime position of Bath is vividly demonstrated by the contour map. The river Avon slices through the limestone plateau of the southern Cotswolds cutting a steep-sided valley to the east of Bathampton Down but the valley widens out downstream from Bath. The place where the city grew up was at a spot where the river could be most easily crossed – the hills on either side were not too steep and the valley floor not too wide or marshy. An added advantage was that the river was easily navigable to this point. (Source: author).

at Bristol. Recent research has shown that rain falling up to ten thousand years ago on the Mendips seeped slowly down the sloping bedding planes of the Carboniferous limestone to a depth of between 2700 and 4300 m, where the natural heart of the earth's core raised its temperature to within the range 64–96C. It is possible that even older water from the underlying Devonian sandstones may have filtered up to join the main reservoir in the Carboniferous limestone. The seepage down and the heating took a long time – many thousands of years – but the ascent to the surface along a major thrust fault in the limestone was rapid. Some of the rising thermal water was trapped in the overlying Triassic marls and sandstones which served as an aquifer, allowing the water to spread laterally beneath the impervious shales, marls and clays of the Lower

2. Section through the geology of north Somerset. Rain which fell on the Mendips ten thousand or so years ago sank down along the bedding plains and joints of the Carboniferous limestone where it was heated by the natural heat of the earth's core. At intervals it could rise, under pressure, through fault lines and reach the horizontally bedded Triassic rocks nearer the surface. Other fault lines through the Triassic marl and the overlying Jurassic clays and limestone allowed the water, under pressure, to reach the surface to appear as springs. The principal fault line ran through Bath. (Source: redrawn after Andrews et all 1982, fig. 4).

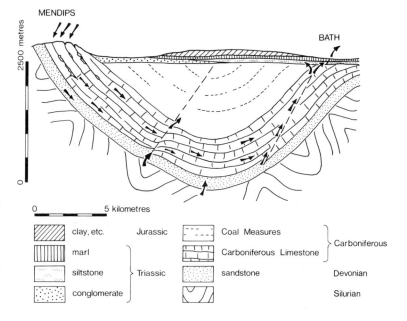

Lias series which formed the floor of the valley of Bath. Only where these strata were faulted could the thermal water, under considerable pressure, reach the surface. One such line of weakness, known as the Penny Quick fault, passes through Bath, and along fissures in this zone of weakness the waters make their final ascent to become the hot springs of Bath, emerging at the King's Bath at 46C, at the Hot Bath at 49C, and at the Cross Bath at 40C. It is an amusing thought that the rain which dropped on the Mendips while the Mesolithic hunters were sheltering in the woods around the Bath spring is the spring water now rising to the surface.

We can assume, then, that the hot springs rising out of the clay ridge in a bend in the Avon valley have been a feature of the landscape for at least the last 10,000 years or so. Such a remarkable phenomenon cannot have failed to have impressed itself upon the superstitious minds of the prehistoric inhabitants of the region. The grandeur of the setting, with the great curve of the river containing and defining the thickly wooded slope from which issued two rivulets of steaming water, would have been a familiar, if awesome, sight – somewhere, surely forbidden to ordinary men, where the gods dwelt. And for those bold enough to penetrate the tangled wood to its heart there would have been an even more remarkable scene – the bubbling waters gushing upwards through black quicksands fringed by matted vegetation and boulders, all bright red, stained by the oxidized iron salts in the water. It was an intensity of colour quite unusual in the dun-toned world of prehistoric man, a red seen only when a beast or being was freshly slaughtered. The genteel setting of the spring today, tamed by the strains of the Pump Room trio and constricted within elegant Bathstone facades, somewhat hinders the imagination but to gain some impression of the sheer terror which these ancient sacred places could inspire, even in comparatively hard-headed people like the Romans, one has only to read the Roman poet Lucan's description of a sacred grove in Gaul, near Toulouse.

'A grove there was, untouched by men's hands from ancient times, whose interlacing boughs enclosed a space of darkness and cold shade, and banished the sunlight far above. No rural Pan dwelt there, no Silvanus, ruler of the woods, no Nymphs; but gods were worshipped there with savage rites, the altars were heaped with hideous offerings, and every tree was sprinkled with human gore. On those boughs ... birds feared to perch; in those coverts wild beasts would not lie down; no wind ever bore down upon that wood, nor thunderbolt hurled from black clouds; the trees, even when they spread their leaves to no breeze, rustled of themselves. Water, also, fell there in abundance from dark springs. The images of the gods, grim and rude, were uncouth blocks formed of felled tree-trunks. Their mere antiquity and the ghastly hue of their rotten timber struck terror .... Legend also told that often the subterranean hollows quaked and bellowed, that yew-trees fell down and rose again, that the glare of conflagration came from trees that were not on fire, and that serpents

twined and glided round the stems. The people never resorted thither to worship at close quarters, but left the place to the gods'.

The landscape around Bath was intensively used in the prehistoric period. The upland plateaux around are densely scattered with flint implements of the Neolithic and Early Bronze Age suggesting the presence of settlements, yet to be defined in precise terms by excavation. Monuments to the Bronze Age dead can still be seen as scattered *tumuli* on Lansdown, Charmy Down and Bathampton Down but such prominent earthworks have suffered much from looting in the past and other depredations more recently. On Charmy Down, for example, there were once two groups of barrows. Several were ransacked by local amateurs in 1822 in the manner of the time. The Revd. Skinner gives the flavour by recording in his diary, 'Soon after breakfast Mr. Conybeare despatched labourers to open a tumulus on Charney (*sic*) Down . . .'. The damage caused was irreparable but at least the bulk of the barrows remained until the Second World War when they were totally flattened to make way for an airfield. Fortunately, however, skilful excavation in advance of destruction produced a range of grave goods including pottery, a bronze dagger knife, beads of shale and jet, and a decorated shale ring – together indicating something of the status of the Bronze Age occupants.

3. The early barrow excavation on Lansdown produced a fragile, but once fine 'Sun-disc' made of gold, 17.25 cm in diameter. The central motif is reminiscent of a solar symbol and must reflect the importance of the sun to the local community in the period 1400–1200 BC. The sun symbol recurs again many times in the Roman sculpture associated with the Temple of Sulis Minera.

The barrows on Lansdown fared less well, most of them being dug over, in an appalling destructive manner, by local Edwardian antiquaries. One produced a remarkable gilded bronze disc decorated in repousee style with what must surely be an emblem representing the sun (ill. 3). These sun discs have occasionally turned up in Bronze Age contexts elsewhere in Europe but the proximity of the Lansdown disc to the sacred spring with its solar iconography – albeit manifesting itself 1500 years later in the Roman temple – is, at least, suggestive of a long continuity.

Apart from the barrows and scatters of flints there is little yet that can be said of the Neolithic and Earlier Bronze Age settlement in the Bath region but from the first half of the first millennium BC the picture of prehistoric activity begins to become clearer. In the eighth-seventh centuries – the period

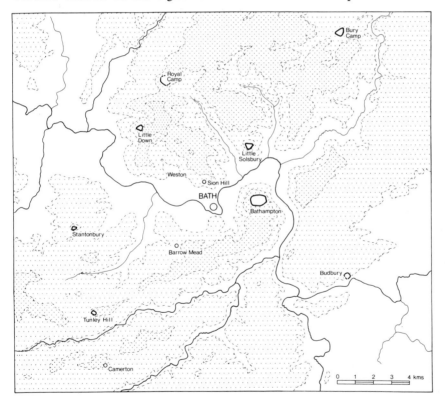

4.   There are a number of pre-Roman Iron Age sites in the Bath region. Most of those known are hillforts built and used at various times in the period 800–100 BC. Budbury and Bathampton are early in this period, Little Solsbury is later but had probably gone out of use by the third or second century BC. The latest and most strongly defended fort is Bury Camp which was probably abandoned soon after 100 BC. In the immediate vicinity of Bath, just to the west of the city, evidence of a late Iron Age settlement has been found which dates to just before the Roman conquest. (Source: Cunliffe & Davenport 1985, fig. 2)

during which iron technology began to be introduced – several defended settlements were constructed in the Bath region (ill. 4). One of these, at Budbury near Bradford on Avon, was a small but strongly defended ridge-end enclosure which, judging from the considerable quantity of domestic rubbish yielded during excavation, is most likely to have been a settlement of high status. Some 6 km away to the north-west was a broadly contemporary enclosure occupying 33 ha of the end of the Bathampton ridge. Limited excavation has shown it to have been defended by a wall 3 m thick fronted by a shallow ditch. These very large hilltop enclosures are something of a mystery, not least because none have been adequately excavated but the general impression gained from limited trial trenching is that they were not inhabited on any scale. One possibility is that the settings of four posts found in some of them were fodder racks and the purpose of the earthworks was to provide a protected environment for the communities' flocks and herds at certain times during the year when they were brought together for culling, castration or redistribution.

Budbury and Bathampton can both be dated roughly to the eighth to sixth centuries BC and represent the first communal settlement architecture in the region. For this reason they can be said to be the beginnings of a tradition of settlement which eventually led to the development of Bath.

The next stage, broadly sixth to second centuries BC, is represented by the hillfort of Little Solsbury occupying a triangular-shaped plateau overlooking the Avon 4 km north-east of Bath (ill. 5). Once more excavation has been on a very limited scale, but sufficient to show that the 8 ha enclosure was defended by a rampart 6.5 m thick, faced inside and out by drystone walling. Inside the fort traces of post-built houses, hearths and a quantity of domestic rubbish suggest quite intensive occupation over a period of time by a farming community growing wheat and breeding sheep on a large scale. The discovery of several weaving combs and a number of spindle whorls is an indication of the importance of wool production – one of the staple industries of the Bath region into the later Middle Ages. Yet in spite of the impression of rural simplicity which archaeological evidence so often gives, the massiveness of the defences, and the discovery of horse gear and spears, provide a reminder of the war-like nature of Iron Age society.

When and how the occupation of Little Solsbury came to an end is at present uncertain, and will remain so until an adequate modern excavation is undertaken on the hill, but on present evidence there is nothing which *need* date to after the third century BC and the lack of elaboration of the defences may imply early abandonment. One possibility is that the site was eclipsed in importance by the great multivallate hillfort of Bury Wood Camp 8 km to the north-east, where occupation lasted at least to the first century BC. Fascinating though the problems are, there can be no certainty about the rise and fall of these nucleated defended settlements until there has been further excavation nor, at present, can anything worthwhile be said of the status of the forts to the west of Bath: Royal Camp, Little Down, Stantonbury and Tunley Hill.

5.   The hillfort on Little Solsbury Hill dominates Bath. Limited excavation has shown that the hilltop was defended by a wide rampart faced by drystone walls and fronted by a ditch. The fort seems to have been heavily occupied in the period *c.* 500–200 BC. Ploughing in the medieval period has obscured the Iron Age features inside the ramparts.

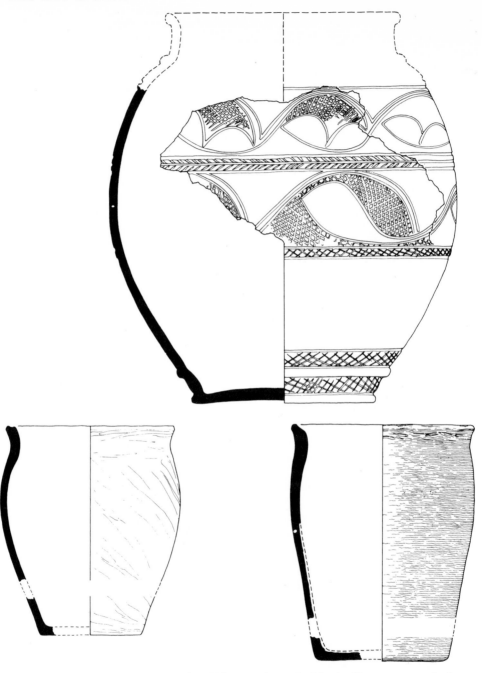

6.   An Iron Age settlement was discovered on Sion Hill, just to the north of the city. No proper excavation has yet been carried out but a small collection of pottery was recovered including a fine highly-decorated jar ornamented in Celtic curvilinear style. Vessels of this kind are generally known as Glastonbury ware though the type is now known to have been widely made in south-west Britain. Scale 1:3. (Source: Cunliffe 1979, fig. 59).

In addition to the hilltop defended sites which, whatever their precise dates, must reflect the communal effort of a significant sector of the population, there would also have been a large number of farmsteads, occupied by families or extended families, scattered about the countryside on the lower, more fertile, slopes. In the vicinity of Bath only two settlements, at Sion Hill and Barrow Mead, have been partially examined but very many more must exist and remain to be discovered (ills. 4 and 6).

One particularly interesting chance find was made in 1864 or 5 at Weston in what was once a secluded valley to the west of Bath. At a depth of 2 m below the bank of Locks Brook a pair of decorated bronze spoons were discovered (ill. 7). They are of a rare type – Iron Age in date – found only in the British Isles and northern France, usually in watery contexts such as bogs or streams. Frequently they occur in pairs, one with a cross in the bowl, the other with a small hole perforated in one edge. Such curious objects are most likely to have had some ritual connotation and their predominantly watery find-spots suggest that many of them ended up as votive offerings to local water deities. Nothing more is known of the site at Weston. The spoons could have been a casual, one-off, deposit but the possibility remains that the stream was revered in the Iron Age and there may be much more to be discovered.

The Weston find brings us back to a consideration of the Bath springs in the pre-Roman Iron Age. Is there any positive evidence that they too were the scene of ritual activity before the Roman conquest? Before we can approach the question it is necessary to try to peel off the overburden of recent, medieval, Saxon and Roman Bath to see what the landscape looked like at this crucial moment at the beginning of the city's history. The last 2000 years have considerably modified the appearance of the land. Massive levelling operations in the Roman period, the accretion of up to 6 m of stratified building- and rubbish-deposits since then, and extensive manipulation of the River Avon, have all contributed to disguise the late Iron Age land scape, but painstaking research by Dr. Geoffrey Kellaway, using evidence from boreholes and excavations, has enabled a detailed picture of the geomorphology of the site to be built up (ill. 8).

The area of Bath later to be walled and to form the nucleus of the city was divided into two by an ancient E–W valley – roughly the line of the present Westgate Street. To the north the land rose steeply in the form of a bluff 6 m or so high, to flatten out for a distance before the rise to Lansdown began. South of the Westgate Street valley were two small knolls of clay projecting

7. Two bronze spoons decorated in Celtic (Iron Age) style were found in a stream bed at Weston in 1867. Pairs of spoons of this kind have been found from time to time in Britain, usually in ritual contexts. The Weston spoons may signify a sacred place. Scale 1:2

above the alluvial deposits of the main valley bottom and separated by another valley in which flowed the outfall from the King's Bath spring. In the crest of the western knoll the Cross Bath and Hetling springs emerged, their outfall dispersing through another valley to join the Avon further downstream. Since their combined flow was considerably less than that of the King's Bath spring the outfall valley was comparatively slighter.

The Avon flowed in a wide valley between 150 and 400 m wide floored with alluvium. For the most part it would have been treacherous to cross, except just to the north of where Pulteney bridge now stands where the steep cliff between Walcot Street and the Paragon faces a low, well-drained gravel hillock (occupied now by Henrietta Park). Here the crossing was narrow, barely 40 m. It would have been far easier to paddle across between the firm banks at this point than to attempt to find a way across the wide marshy flood plain, tangled with vegetation, to the south.

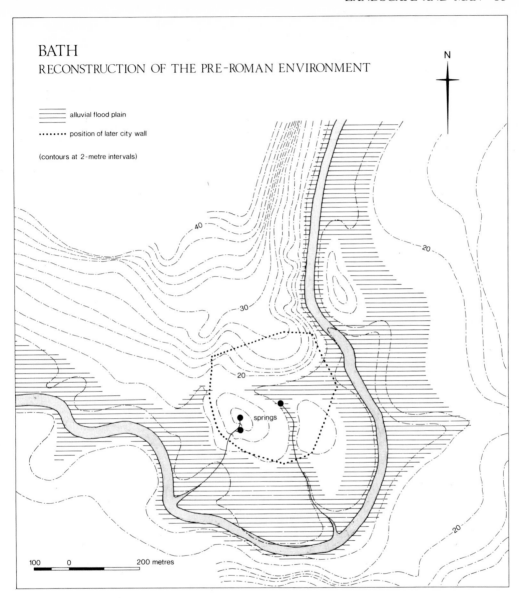

BATH
RECONSTRUCTION OF THE PRE-ROMAN ENVIRONMENT

N

≡≡≡ alluvial flood plain

•••••• position of later city wall

(contours at 2-metre intervals)

springs

100   0   200 metres

8. A detailed idea of the landscape of Bath before the Romans has been built up by Dr. Geoffrey Kellaway using evidence from boreholes and other observations of the subsoil. The map shows the wide extent of the alluvium of the valley floor and the two streams leading from the two groups of springs to the river. North of the King's Bath spring in the centre the land rises quite steeply. (Source: redrawn version of a map by G.A. Kellaway in Cunliffe & Davenport 1985, fig. 1).

So much for the setting, but what of the springs themselves? It is only at the King's Bath spring where extensive excavations have recently been completed that we have some knowledge of the pre-Roman situation. The spring arose at one side of an east-west valley (which may itself be a reflection of the ancient fault line). Trial boreholes have shown that the water rises in a funnel-shaped spring pipe eroded into the Lower Lias clay. Because of its low-lying position periodic flooding by the Avon has continuously carried sand and gravel detritus into the spring pipe. It is through this that the thermal waters rise. The edges of the pool were quite hard and solid where the gravel and boulders had been left uneroded by the force of the water, but inwards from this, towards the actual spring head, was an expanse of treacherous deep black mud. The overall size of the spring between the gravel banks was between 20 and 30 m, the closest, safe, approach being on the south side where the gravel bank came to within 4 m or so of the spring head.

Roman building works drastically modified the spring and around the point of inflow the Roman engineers removed a considerable volume of sand and mud, but some of the original deposit has washed in, bringing with it a number of flint implements of Mesolithic and Neolithic date. Yet such was the pressure of the water that the silt accumulating in the Roman period, and the votive offerings thrown in, were churned up with the earlier prehistoric material. From this quicksand filling, amid a mass of Roman material, were recovered 18 Celtic silver or silver-plated coins: a Gaulish minim, a quarter-stater of the Durotriges and seven silver coins of the Dobunni, the tribe who occupied what is now Gloucestershire and northern Somerset (ill. 9). The problem posed is, were these coins

9. Celtic coins from the sacred spring possibly thrown into the waters in the pre-Roman period. 1, a silver quarter stater of the Durotriges (a Dorset tribe); 2, a silver stater, Class F, of the Dobunni; 3, an inscribed silver stater of the Dobunni bearing the name Anted. The Dobunni occupied Gloucestershire and north Somerset. Anted was one of the rulers or magistrates. (Scale 2:1).

1   2   3

thrown in in the pre-Roman period as offerings from the local Celtic population or were they still in circulation in the early Roman period and deposited then? On balance the relatively fresh and unworn appearance of most of the pieces suggests Iron Age deposition. The tantalizing reality is that we will never know for certain.

Celtic reverence for the natural settings of sacred locations would suggest that little if anything was done to modify the environs of the Bath springs. In all probability they lay remote in their dark and tangled woodland. Certainly no evidence of Iron Age structural activity has been found but then so little of the contemporary surface has yet been examined in the vicinity of the spring. It may, however, be significant that nowhere within the later walled area of the city has any trace of pre-Roman occupation been found, yet to the west at Sion Hill and at the Lower Common below Royal Victoria Park traces of an Iron Age settlement have recently been identified. One tempting hypothesis is that the area around the springs – perhaps even the area enclosed by the later Roman wall – was regarded as sacred to the deity and was left in its natural state untainted by human interference, much in the manner of the sacred grove in Gaul described by Lucan. These are fascinating questions upon which future excavations may eventually throw some light but whatever the true situation one thing is clear – with the coming of the Roman army in AD 43 the mysterious calm of the ancient sanctuary was to be shattered.

2. AQUAE SULIS: THE ROMAN SPA

IN LATE SUMMER AD 43 the Roman army under the command of Aulus Plautius landed in Kent to begin the subjugation of Britain. The advance was rapid and by the end of the campaigning season, or early in the next year, the south-east of the country was under Roman control up to the Severn-Trent line. It seems that at this early stage the Roman strategy was to secure only the south-east, leaving the rest of the island to its own devices, and to this end the army began to construct a frontier zone roughly following the line of the Jurassic limestone hills, and the old cross-country track, from Lyme Bay to the Humber. As an integral part of the frontier installations the military engineers laid out a great linking highway – the Fosse Way – facilitating the movement of troops and supplies, and at intervals along it, usually at important route junctions, forts were built to house military detachments whose job it was to guard and control the crossing points and to act as a strategic reserve when required (ill. 10).

The Fosse Way crossed the River Avon somewhere in the vicinity of Bath and such a significant junction must surely have been garrisoned in the early years of the occupation (ill. 11). The problems facing us therefore are: what line did the early Fosse Way take and where was the fort sited? It must be admitted that there are, as yet, no firm answers, but a number of clues exist and are worth following up. In the first place the Roman engineers would have chosen the simplest and most strategically sensible route. Now, the line of the Fosse is well established to the north of Bath on Banner Down and to the south at Combe Hay, but between all is guesswork. The most likely possibility would be to suppose that the original road from the north ran along the line of London Road through Walcot (the course certainly taken by a major Roman road later) and from there turned to the south-west, crossing the river somewhere roughly in the vicinity of Green Park Station or a little further to the west, thus completely bypassing the area later to become the walled area of *Aquae Sulis*. However a recent discovery has raised another interesting possibility. In the very centre of the city, beneath the buildings on the north side of Bath Street, a massively constructed Roman road has been discovered pre-dating the layout of the temple in the 60s AD (ill. 20). The road must therefore date to the very earliest phase of the Roman occupation and its solid construction suggests military work. The line runs diagonally across the city from Hot Bath Street to Northgate. Could this be the original military Fosse Way? It would line up remarkably well with the known

course of the road at Combe Hay (though there may have been deviations between to circumnavigate deep coombs). From Northgate the course may have followed Walcot Street to London Road, or have crossed the river just above Pulteney Bridge.

The Walcot Street area may indeed have been an important cross roads at this time upon which converged three other roads: one coming from the south-east from Poole Harbour, one from the east, ultimately from London, and one from the west from the military supply base and later port at Sea Mills on the mouth of the Avon. There may also have been a fourth road coming from the north-west across Lansdown. Exactly where they converged and where the main river crossing lay is completely unknown but the narrowness of the valley just above Pulteney Bridge and the firm gravel elevation in the Henrietta Park region of Bathwick might suggest a crossing point somewhere between Pulteney and Cleveland Bridges.

From what has been said, it is evident that Bath was at a crucial node in the communication network of the early frontier system. Such a location would certainly have been garrisoned but we cannot expect the picture to have been simple. Exca-

10. Air view of the line of the Fosse Way at Stratton-on-the-Fosse near Downside Abbey. The modern road closely follows the line of the Roman highway.

vations at Cirencester and Gloucester have shown that forts had limited lives and could be relocated in response to troop movements reflecting the constantly changing military situation: so it probably was at Bath.

One site, however, commends itself as a most likely Roman choice – the elevated gravel terrace at Bathwick close to the river and commanding one of the major crossing points. There is no positive archaeological evidence to prove the suggestion but the discovery of early samian pottery of the correct date from the area is at least mildly encouraging. Another possible location may be suggested to the west of the city below Royal Crescent and Victoria Park where some scraps of early material have recently come to light. But evidence is sparse and the question of the location of the early military base (or bases) must remain open.

The Early Roman military presence can be demonstrated in a more graphic way. In the eighteenth and early nineteenth centuries development in the Walcot area, along London Road, brought to light evidence of one of the early cemeteries of Bath including a number of military tombstones (ill. 12). Some of these commemorate soldiers who retired to Bath long after the army had moved away to fight in more distant parts of the country, but a few seem to belong to men who died on active service in the region. Two of them were of cavalrymen, one of whom, L. Vitellius Tancinus, served with a unit called the *ala*

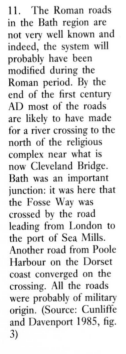

11. The Roman roads in the Bath region are not very well known and indeed, the system will probably have been modified during the Roman period. By the end of the first century AD most of the roads are likely to have made for a river crossing to the north of the religious complex near what is now Cleveland Bridge. Bath was an important junction: it was here that the Fosse Way was crossed by the road leading from London to the port of Sea Mills. Another road from Poole Harbour on the Dorset coast converged on the crossing. All the roads were probably of military origin. (Source: Cunliffe and Davenport 1985, fig. 3)

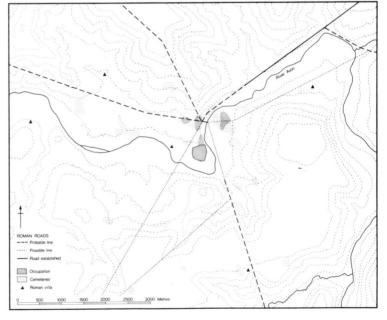

Vettonum. Two others were put up by legionaries, Antigonus and M. Valerius Latinus, both of the *Legio XX*. If all four do belong to the early military phase they indicate that the garrison may have changed more than once, since it would be unusual for legionaries and auxiliaries to be garrisoned together.

Apart from the tombstones the one really tangible piece of archaeological evidence for the early military phase of Bath is the length of massively constructed Roman road found beneath the temple precinct in the centre of the town. Is its siting due to purely practical considerations or is there more to it than that? The road slashes straight through what would have been the heart of the Celtic sanctuary dislocating the King's Bath spring from the Cross Bath and Hetling springs – the equivalent to building a motorway through Wells Cathedral precinct! Such an act of imperial arrogance may have been carefully calculated to destroy, decisively, the mysteries surrounding the ancient cult centre.

The army presence would have lasted for about 20 years or so before the troops moved on to new theatres of war in Wales and the north. But the army base and the excellent new system of communications would have drawn camp followers and local traders to the crossing and there many of them would have settled in an ill-organized *vicus* providing services for the garrison and a market for the local country dwellers. Very little structural evidence survives of this early (pre-Flavian) period (i.e. AD 43–69) but collections of Roman pottery, recovered during building work, together with limited archaeological investigation, give some idea of the extent of the first settlement. Pre-Flavian pottery has been found in three areas: in Bathwick, along the London Road in Walcot and beneath Citizen House (Westgate Buildings) within the walled area of the city. At this last site fragments of painted wall plaster from a lathe and plaster wall show that there were quite elaborate timber buildings in existence at the time – these are the earliest Roman buildings known on the site of Bath and lie at the very beginnings of the city's urban development.

The spread of settlement, on either side of the river around the crossing point, and stretching southwards to the general area of the springs, sets the scene for the next two centuries or so of development (ill. 20). We know nothing about the organizational layout of the settlement but in all probability it was an *ad hoc* arrangement of shops with stalls in the front and living quarters behind, facing the main roads, and divided by side and back alleys – the organic arrangement of a *vicus* rather than the regular chequer-board grid of a cantonal capital. How

12. Tombstones of Roman soldiers from the cemetery along the Fosse Way just north of Bath. The two figured pieces are from different tombstones both showing Roman cavalrymen trampling down an enemy. The inscribed panel beneath the larger fragment reads 'Lucius Vitellius Tancinus, son of Mantaius, a tribesman of Caurium in Spain, trooper of the cavalry regiment of Vettones. Roman citizen, aged 46, of 26 years service, lies buried here'.

The complete unfigured tombstone reads 'Julius Vitalis, armourer of the Twentieth Legion Valeria Victrix, of 9 years service, aged 29, a Belgic tribesman, with funeral at the cost of the Guild of Armourers: he lies here'.

the sacred springs fared during this time we do not know. It is inconceivable that they did not continue to be revered, but no trace of early aggrandizement has been discovered. Whatever there may have been was swept away in the great programme of monumentalizing which began in the 60s of the first century AD.

Before considering this remarkable phenomenon something must be said of the political situation in the new province of Britannia. In AD 60 a rebellion broke out in eastern Britain led by the Icenian queen Boudica. There were many reasons for native discontent but they centred upon the great temple to the deified emperor Claudius set up in the centre of the old tribal capital at Camulodunum (Colchester). To put up such a building was an ill-judged act of arrogance on the part of the Roman administrators. They must have thought it would provide a new national focus for the native population but to the locals it was a gross provocation.

The rebellion when it came was widespread and bloody. London, Colchester and Verulamium were burnt and troubles extended even into the south-west, but the dissidents were eventually routed and put down by the relentless skill of Roman arms. For the next decade the ravaged province settled down to lick its wounds while a new generation of skilled administrators looked for ways to heal the rift and to build confidence among the local populace. It is at this stage that the ancient native sanctuary at Bath, disfigured by ill-considered development in the early years of the occupation, was subjected to one of the most elaborate building programmes the province had known to become the world-famous Temple of Sulis Minerva.

Whilst it is impossible for us ever to know who was responsible for the first monumentalizing of Bath, and what their motives were, the sheer scale of the work and the fact that it was carried out in the decade of reconciliation (AD 60–70) would argue for official involvement. The old Celtic shrine of Sulis was suddenly taken in hand and, cleared of its clutter, emerged resplendent as the sanctuary of Sulis Minerva complete with a temple in classical style, set within a spacious precinct, and a vast suite of baths where pilgrims could immerse themselves in the sacred thermal waters (ills. 14 and 17). It was quite possibly at this time that Bath was given its first recorded name *Aquae Sulis* – the waters of Sulis. The  appearance of the Roman goddess Minerva is interesting. It was quite normal Roman practice for native deities to be conflated with their nearest Roman equivalent to make the abilities of the deity more familiar to those unacquainted with local tradition.

Minerva, in her guise of goddess of wisdom, with curative powers and a certain martial prowess, no doubt closely reflected the nature of the native Sulis. Henceforth, as Sulis Minerva, the deity would represent a kind of universality which underpinned the Roman world – she was in many ways a symbol of the unification of Roman and native. The decision to aggrandize such a symbol in monumental architecture, the like of which was hardly yet known in the province, could well have been the deliberate act of a shrewd colonial administrator.

In its original conception the temple complex presented an aspect of simple, even stark, elegance. The temple itself – a small tetrastyle (four-columned) building in the Corinthian order – stood on a high podium towards the centre of a large colonnaded precinct 52 m by 70 m. In front of it, to the east, lay the sacrificial altar set in the middle of an area paved with massive slabs of Lias limestone. The temple, altar and eastern entrance were all carefully aligned on an east to west axis. This simple arrangement was interrupted only in the south-east corner where the sacred spring rose. Here the mud and rubble

13. The taming of the spring was a major feat of engineering. The spring head was surrounded by a ring of driven piles to consolidate the ground. Mud was then removed from within and the general water-level lowered through a specially dug overflow ditch. The next stage involved the digging of a foundation trench outside the stabilizing piles. The base of this was piled and then the construction of the reservoir wall could begin using massive stone blocks. (Source: Cunliffe & Davenport 1985, fig. 21).

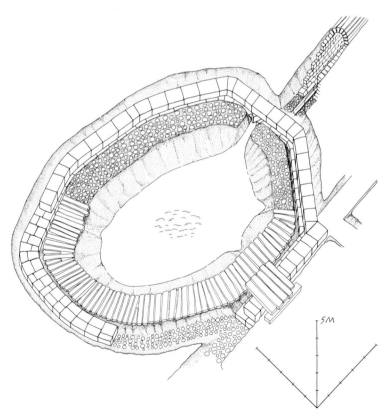

5M

Period 1

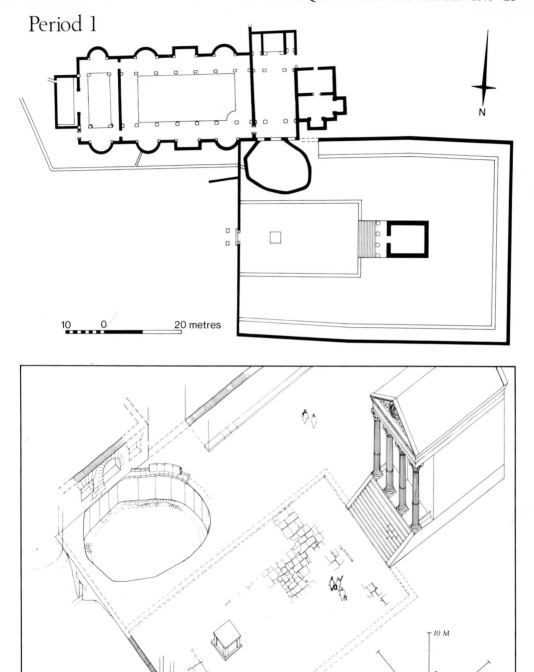

N

10   0   20 metres

S.G.

14.   The baths and the Temple of Sulis Minerva were laid out together in the 60's or 70's of the first century AD. At this stage the spring was an open pool in the corner of the temple precinct. The temple fronted on to a paved area on the main axis of which stood the sacrificial altar. (Source: plan, author; axonometric, Sheila Gibson).

surrounding the natural spring head had been removed and the
fissures through which the hot water emerged were entirely
surrounded by a wall lined internally with lead to form a
watertight tank or reservoir 2 m deep (ill. 13).

The skill of the hydraulic engineers was impressive. They
must have realized that one of the most serious problems with
which they had to contend was the fact that the water constantly
brought up a mass of black sand from deep in its spring pipe.
Their problem therefore was threefold: to create a pool visually
acceptable in the context of the temple; to provide a head of
water sufficient to feed the thermal baths to the south; and to
arrange the system in such a way that the sand brought up by the
spring would not clog everything up. The method they adopted
was elegant in its simplicity. In the east wall of the reservoir they
created a sluice slot, closed by a movable sluice, and joined to
the head of a very substantial drain. For the most part the sluice
would have been closed keeping the water-level high to feed the
baths. Throughout this time sand would have built up. When it
was judged that the depth of sand had reached the acceptable
limit all that had to be done was to open the sluice allowing the
head of water to flush all the sediment out into the drainage
system. The flow of water would have been sufficient to clear
the system but in the event of blockage the drain had been
constructed sufficiently large, and with regular manholes, to
allow men with shovels access to move any impediment. Once
flushed out the sluice would be closed and the reservoir could
fill again in two or three days.

Describing the sacred spring in these practical terms may
highlight the brilliance of Bath's first city engineer but it all
sounds rather mundane. In fact the spring was nothing of the
kind: it was a place of great mystery – an awesome spot where
the unfathomable underworld of the gods communicated with
the world of mortals. It was here that the presiding deity could
be approached. She could be asked favours but she demanded
propitiation. The excavation in the spring threw a vivid light on
these beliefs and practices. Messages to Sulis Minerva,
inscribed on plaques of lead and pewter, usually asking her to
punish enemies, were recovered in some number together with
an impressive array of offerings; 12,000 coins, libation vessels of
pewter, bronze and silver, and a variety of other trinkets. The
power of the deity was considerable and no-one would have
approached her spring lightly (ill. 18).

If the spring had an aura of sanctity, it was the temple itself
which physically dominated the scene. Set high on the podium
and fronted by a flight of steps, the building towered above its

15. The life-sized gilded bronze head of Minerva was found in a sewer trench in Stall Street in 1727. The statue, complete with a high Corinthian helmet, was probably the cult statue once standing in the temple.

surroundings while its richly decorated front – four large Corinthian columns supporting the famous Gorgon's head pediment – commanded the attention of all (ill. 17). It was here that the cult figure of the goddess and the sacred objects of the temple were kept in a setting appropriate to her power (ill. 15).

The temple complex was only one element of Bath's first monumental ensemble. To the south lay the baths – one of the other essential components of a great healing shrine. That the two complexes were integral is clearly demonstrated by the wall they shared in common forming, at the same time, the south side of the spring and the north wall of an entrance hall. This wall, with its three great openings visually linking temple and baths, can still, in part, be seen. Today visitors peer through it to view the spring, hardly aware that the massive carefully-jointed stone blocks of the curved and joggled arches represent one of the most impressive examples of Roman building standing in Britain. Through these openings visitors to the baths in the first century AD would have been given an incomparable view across the spring to the altar beyond, while those in the precinct would have been able to see into the great hall of the bathing

16. Fragments from the pediment of the Temple of Sulis Minerva found beneath the Pump Room over the last 300 years. (Source: Cunliffe & Davenport 1985, fig. 11). The central motif – the great 'Gorgon's Head' – glowered down on Roman worshippers for nearly four centuries.

establishment which divided the small rooms of the artificially heated suite from the Great Bath, and two smaller pools, together constituting a series of thermal swimming baths. There can be little doubt that the first temple and the first baths were planned together, to be interlinked visually and functionally, as part of a single scheme.

Such an arrangement occurs sporadically throughout the Roman world and is typical of curative shrines where bathing in the sacred waters was an essential part of the ritual of cleansing and curing. But these shrines were also places of social contact where comfort and pleasure were to be had – not at all unlike a modern health farm. They were also places where religious performances would be staged, usually in specially constructed theatres. At present no such building is known in Bath but one ought to exist somewhere below the modern streets. The only possible clue is provided by several blocks of a richly ornamented cornice carved with lions' heads which were found beneath the floor of a cellar in Westgate Street just north of the temple. A theatre hereabouts could have made use of the steep

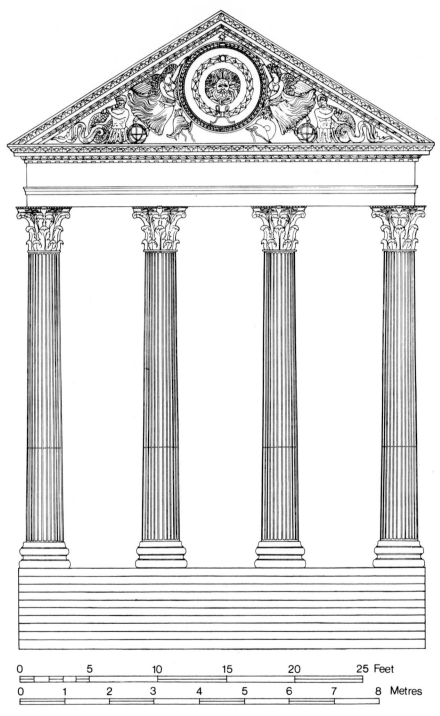

17. The front of the Temple of Sulis Minerva.

18.   Votive offerings from the sacred spring. Top left: penannular brooch in copper alloy with inset red enamel in the terminals. Top right: one of the pewter curses. Bottom: two pewter and one silver vessel for pouring libations. On the handle of one can clearly be seen the inscription DEAE SUL MIN – 'to the goddess Sulis Minerva'.

19. The Great Bath dominated the bathing establishment. In the Roman period it was always roofed, first with timber and later with a massive masonry vault. The bath was, and still is, lined with sheets of lead seen here when the bath was emptied.

rise in the ground. Digging away bedrock to provide for the curving tiers of seats would have been preferable to building the structure up in massively buttressed masonry. All this is, however, speculation and we must await tangible evidence before the problem of Bath's first theatre can be resolved.

The complex of monumental buildings – temple, baths and possible theatre, planned with precision, built in masonry and ornamented with richly carved reliefs – was quite unlike anything the youthful province had experienced. Indeed it is highly unlikely that the necessary skills would have existed in Britain at the time except among the army and the gangs of skilled craftsmen brought in on contract work. In all probability the Bath sanctuary was built by native labourers learning totally new skills from north Gaulish craftsmen, themselves building to a brief drawn up by military engineers.

Once created the temple and baths dominated the Roman settlement. But buildings need maintenance and fashions change and from time to time a wealthy patron or a local authority desires to make a mark by providing improved facilities. Thus it was in the centre of *Aquae Sulis*.

Some time in the early second century, quite possibly during the reign of Hadrian, it seems that a new precinct was laid out to the east of the main temple precinct (ill. 21). Its corner survives but the rest lies inaccessibly beneath the present Abbey. In such a central position, however, it is most likely to have contained a

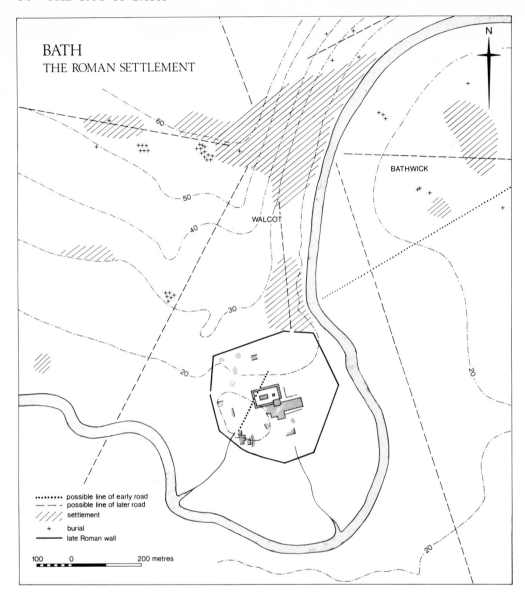

BATH
THE ROMAN SETTLEMENT

BATHWICK

WALCOT

········· possible line of early road
— · — · possible line of later road
///// settlement
+ burial
——— late Roman wall

100   0   200 metres

20. The plan of the Bath region in the Roman period shows four centuries of activity during which time were many changes. It is probable that the first road system, laid out during the military period, crossed the river near Pulteney Bridge and that the fort guarding it lay somewhere in the Bathwick area. After the army moved off, the road system was reorganized on the Cleveland Bridge crossing point leaving the area of the springs free to be developed as a religious sanctuary, the main settlement focussing on a new road junction. Only later, probably in the fourth century, was the 'city' wall built around the main public buildings creating a structure which has restrained the development of the city ever since. (Source: author).

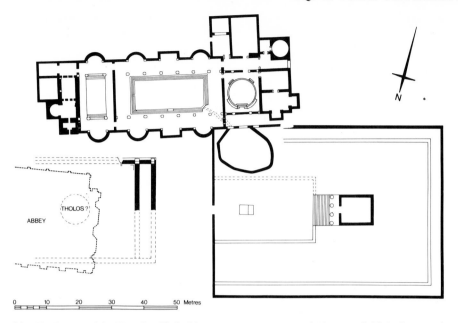

N

ABBEY

THOLOS?

0 10 20 30 40 50 Metres

21.   To the east of the Temple of Sulis Minerva a new precinct was laid out, probably in the second century during the reign of Hadrian. Part of it projects into the present museum but most of it must lie beneath the west end of the abbey.

structure of significance. The vital clue is provided by a number of sculptured blocks found just south of its south-western corner when the baths were first exposed in the 1880s. Taken together these fragments belong to a richly ornamented circular temple, or *tholos*, which is almost certain to have occupied a central position in the new precinct, very probably on the same axis as the Temple of Sulis Minerva. The symmetry of the arrangement is further enhanced by the fact that the diameter of the tholos was almost exactly the same as the width of the main temple.

The new Hadrianic temple was a delicate richly ornamented structure of a kind rare in western Europe though comparatively frequent in the Hellenistic world. A consideration of its carving suggests, once again, the employment of north Gaulish craftsmen. The erection of so exotic a structure – of a type totally unknown elsewhere in Britain – must have been a notable event. One possibility (and it is only an outside guess), is that the temple was occasioned by the visit of the Emperor Hadrian to Britain in 122. Since Hadrian was an ardent admirer of Greek culture the erection of a Hellenistic-inspired tholos, at one of

S G

5   0   5 metres

22.   A number of fragments from a building in the new precinct survive sufficient to show that it was a tholos (circular temple) richly ornamented with sculpture. (Source: Sheila Gibson).

23.   The temple precinct in its most developed form. The precinct floor was originally paved with lias limestone slabs and later repatched around the altar (middle left) with thinner slabs of pennant grit. The two steps (right) led up to a portico in front of the reservoir wall. The rough wall (left) is the wall of the Pump Room built in 1790 on the Roman foundations. At the time much of the Gorgon's Head pediment was found.

the premier native sanctuaries in the province, would have been much in keeping with the spirit of the time and would have appealed to the emperor. Perhaps, one day, excavation will be possible to throw some further light on this tantalizing ill-known monument.

As the years passed the sanctuary was further modified. The most far-reaching changes took place some time around AD 300 when there was a thorough-going reorganization of the entire complex. The temple, now nearly 250 years old, was transformed. The original building was enclosed within a new retaining wall creating a kind of ambulatory around the old building. A new facade, incorporating a flight of steps between two flanking chapels (or shrines), added a grandeur to the approach while in no way detracting from the original tetrastyle Corinthian front. The change is particularly interesting because it converted what had previously been a purely classical arrangement into one far more like the native, Romano-Celtic, style. Perhaps we should see in all this a change in ritual to a rather more local type of religious observance.

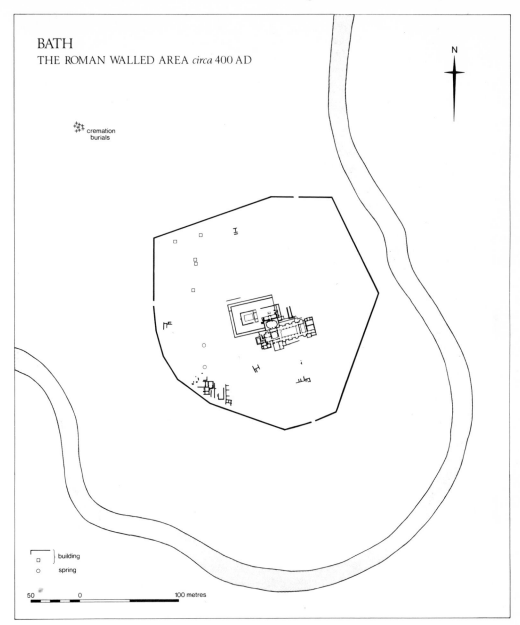

BATH
THE ROMAN WALLED AREA *circa* 400 AD

N

cremation
burials

building
spring

50   0   100 metres

24. Roman Bath was dominated by the great buildings of the sanctuary of Sulis Minerva clustering around the King's Bath spring – the temple, the bathing establishment and the theatre (wherever it was). The other springs would also have been fitted out in some style, the Cross Bath spring probably fed into a large ornamental basin while the Hot Bath spring served another bathing estabishment. Little is known of the rest of the settlement except that a number of the buildings, possibly private houses, were adorned with mosaics. (Source: author).

25. Two sculpted corners of the altar are shown here re-erected on the original altar platform. The block (far left) is an inscription referring to an offering, probably a statue which stood behind it, put up in honour of the goddess Sulis Minerva by the augur Lucius Marcius Memor.

It was at about this time that an even more dramatic change took place: the hitherto open spring was now encased in a massive hall, vaulted in masonry, effectively cutting the spring off from the precinct and restricting the approach to it (ill. 26). The effect would have been to make it an altogether more mysterious place – a vast echoing grotto, green and dank – a gloomy place pervaded with the noise of the constantly bubbling spring relieved only by the occasional squawk of an intrusive bird.

The enclosure and vaulting of the spring was part of an even more extensive programme. In effect the entire bath suite, which had previously been extended, was now reroofed in masonry – a material far more long-lasting than wood in such a steamy atmosphere. The renovation programme was massive, involving the strengthening of all weight-supporting walls and piers. When complete the overall appearance of the building complex was greatly enhanced while the actual ground plan had changed very little.

The sanctuary had, by the beginning of the third century, reached more or less its final form but some time later, in the

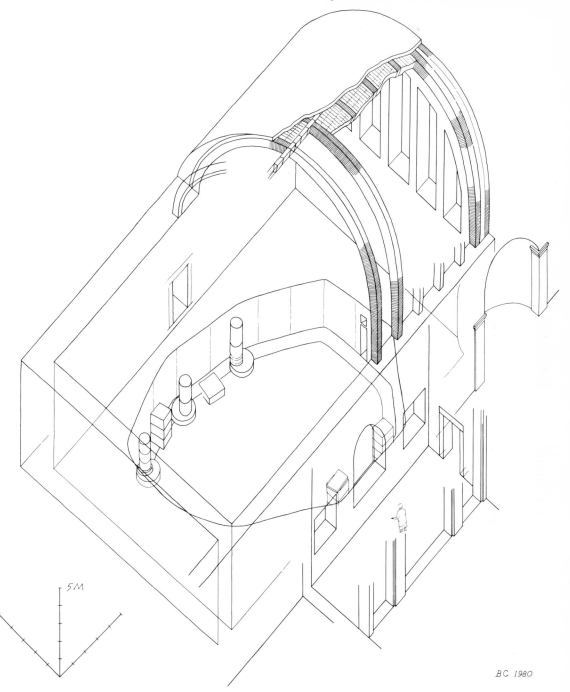

5M

BC 1980

26. The reservoir was enclosed late in the Roman period and roofed with a massive concrete vault.

late third or early fourth century, a modification was made which had a considerable visual effect on the temple precinct. The reservoir enclosure wall had began to subside and crack and to support it a new facade, camouflaging three massive buttresses, was attached to the northern wall of the enclosure (ill. 29). To balance it visually another facade (presumably part of a building) was erected to the north. Both were richly carved, the northern facade incorporating a pediment featuring Luna, the moon

1   0   3 metres

27. In its most developed form the temple precinct was adorned with two buildings facing each other across the sacrificial altar. The Facade of the southern building depicted Sol, god of the sun, representing the southern hemisphere and the day.

goddess, while the southern depicted Sol, god of the sun in the guise of protector of the spring (ills. 27 and 28). The spacing was such that a visitor's view was constrained by the two facades which served to focus attention on the front of the temple. The need to buttress was, then, used as an opportunity to create a totally new visual effect, but it was more than that – the sculptured facades were there to tell a story. Entering the precinct for the first time a visitor would have been confronted with the centrally-placed sacrificial altar its corners carved with well-known deities – Jupiter, Bacchus, Apollo etc. – all small-scale and subservient to the presiding deity (ill. 25). Looking up to the left (south) he would see Sol, protecting the spring and guardian of the light, southern, hemisphere, while to the right (north) was Luna, controller of the dark, northern, hemisphere. Here was the entire cosmos and dominant over all, towering high above, was the pediment of the temple with its fearsome Gorgon's head set against a background of symbols representing the attributes of

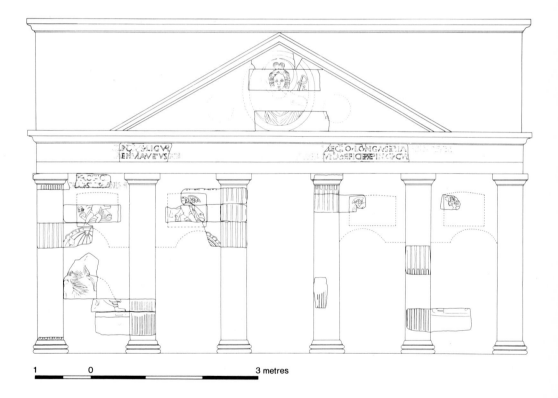

28.   The Facade of the northern building in the temple precinct depicted Luna, goddess of the Moon, representing the northern hemisphere and night. (Source: Author).

Minerva – the owl reminding of her wisdom, the helmets reflecting her military prowess. No-one would be left in any doubt of the power and ascendancy of Sulis Minerva. The precinct in its developed form, then, told the story of the gods fossilized in stone. The full significance of this remarkable monument has only recently been recognized, largely as the result of the excavation programme of 1978–84.

So far we have concentrated upon the central complex of monuments which developed around the King's Bath spring. As the map (ill. 24) will show these occupied a substantial part of the later walled area particularly if the precinct of the tholos and the supposed theatre are allowed for as part of the central complex. The other two springs – the Cross Bath and the Hetling springs – were also in existence in the Roman period and there is some evidence of their use at this time. From deep in the silts clogging the Cross Bath spring have come an altar and a sculptured block depicting scenes from the legend of Aesculapius – the Greco-Roman god of healing. Nothing is yet known of the setting of the spring at this time but it must have been adorned in some way if only as an ornamental pool.

A little to the south is the Hetling spring, which in medieval and more recent times served the Hot Bath. Again the archaeology of the spring has not been explored, but to the south of it, on either side of Hot Bath Street, traces of a substantial Roman bathing establishment have come to light, including a large lead-lined reservoir or swimming bath. The evidence, such as it is, was recorded during building work by local observers in 1864–6 (ill. 30) and again in 1908 and most if not all of the Roman structures will have been destroyed by cellar digging at the time. If our understanding of this part of the sanctuary is still very incomplete we can at least be sure of the existence here of elaborate public buildings occupying a substantial area.

At some stage during the Roman period the principal buildings of the Roman sanctuary were enclosed within a massive wall which it has been conventional to refer to as the first city wall, but this pre-judges the status of the Roman settlement: there is no proof at all that it was a town in the accepted sense of the word. The total enclosed area is about 10 ha (24 acres) which is less than a quarter the size of the average Roman cantonal capital like Silchester or Winchester and substantially smaller than the nearby town of Cirencester. Whatever status *Aquae Sulis* acquired during the Roman period it clearly did not follow the same pattern of development as the cantonal capitals.

Period 3

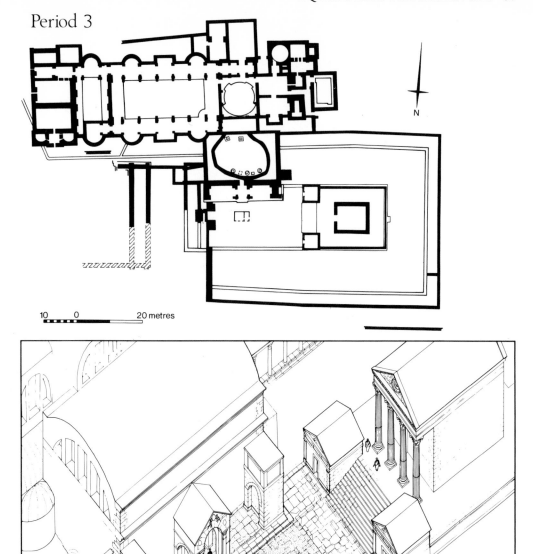

10   0   20 metres

29. By the third century the temple and baths had changed dramatically: the temple had been extended and the reservoir enclosed in a vast vaulted hall. The baths, too, had grown considerably and were also reroofed with masonry vaults. (Source: author and Sheila Gibson).

30. In 1867, when the Royal United Hospital was being built part of a Roman bathing establishment came to light. This is our only evidence to show that the Hot Bath spring was monumentalized by the Romans.

There are two possible explanations for the wall-building: either it was put up as a *temenos* (or boundary) wall to enclose and define the sacred area, or it was built as a defence during the troubled times of the fourth century when a number of smaller settlements like Mildenhall (Wilts.) and Gatcombe (Somerset) were putting up walls to protect their resident communities. On balance the very massiveness of the wall of *Aquae Sulis* would point to a defensive role but the question must remain open.

To date the wall-building is difficult. Although most of it was still standing as late as the beginning of the eighteenth century there is very little now to see apart from a short stretch in Upper Borough Walls, close to the alley leading to Trim Street. A few other lengths are incorporated in later boundary walls along the south-east side but the best stretch, surviving until the late 1950s, was partially demolished and totally obscured by the construction of the modern edifice occupied by Marks and Spencers and Woolworths. That the obliteration of such an important monument was sanctioned without question is a sad comment on the dark age through which Bath was passing at the time. Elsewhere the stump of the wall is buried beneath buildings and streets.

In only one place, in cellars beneath Upper Borough Walls, have the crucial layers behind the wall been examined archaeologically and even here the evidence for dating is ambiguous. At best all that can be said is that it was built late in the Roman period probably after *c*. AD 300. Until that time *Aquae Sulis* was a completely open settlement.

Once built, the wall was to control the development of the city until the eighteenth century, but in the early years the settlement developed without constraint (ill. 20). Evidence of Roman occupation is particularly dense along Walcot Street and includes substantial masonry structures. The settled area certainly spread to the Paragon and along Guinea Lane and Julian Road to behind the Royal Crescent where a Roman street and masonry building were recorded. Further afield Roman buildings and occupation are known along the London Road near Snows Hill, across the river in Bathwick and to the west of the walled area in the region extending from Victoria Park to Green Park Station. How dense was the settlement, and the nature of its planning, if any, are completely unknown but in all probability it was a straggling agglomeration growing up in an *ad hoc* fashion among a network of lanes. It would be wrong to regard this settlement as extra-mural, for much of it was in existence long before the defensive wall was erected. This was *Aquae Sulis* – a sprawl of structures centred on a road and river crossing, dominated by the sanctuary of Sulis Minerva clustering around the three springs.

31. Roman lead seal probably from a bale of wool, found at Combe Down, south of Bath, where the headquarters of an Imperial estate may have been situated. This is the earliest evidence we have of Bath's wool industry which was to become so important to the town's economy in medieval times (scale 4 times life size).

Such an important route nexus would undoubtedly have developed a commercial aspect. Pewter vessels were made in large quantity in the nearby settlements on Lansdown and at Camerton and would have been carted to Bath for sale. Traces of glass-working have been found recently just south of Victoria Park, while inscriptions record a stone-worker (*lapidarius*) and a sculptor – a reminder that high quality building stone is close at hand to the south and east of the town. At a rather more domestic level rubbish from a cobbler's shop was recovered from a pit just outside Northgate. Other products which would certainly have been sold or exchanged in the markets were corn and wool. Very considerable areas of Roman field systems can still be seen on Bathampton Down and Charmy Down and from the Roman settlement on Combe Down came a lead sealing from a bale of wool (ill. 31).

The economy of Roman Bath was probably not at all unlike that of the late medieval city in its heyday as a Cotswold wool town but with one main difference: Roman Bath possessed a shrine, known throughout Europe, which attracted a constant flow of pilgrims bringing wealth and prosperity to the community – a benefit reflected in the outstanding architecture of the sanctuary and also in the fine mosaic pavements found in the domestic buildings dotted around the settlement (ills. 32–3).

The erection of the defensive wall in the fourth century marks a distinct change in the prosperity of the community. There is

32.   Mosaic floors seem to have been quite common in Roman Bath. The floor with the fabulous sea beast was found beneath the Bluecoat School

33. This geometric mosaic floor beneath the Crystal Palace public house.

some evidence to show that some of the areas outside were abandoned, presumably as people began to move into the protection of the walls and it was at about this time that secular buildings began to encroach upon the temple precinct, suggesting perhaps that space was now becoming difficult to find. Certainly, wherever excavation has been possible within the walled area, masonry buildings have been found, implying a dense packing of domestic habitation at this time. Sadly, excavation has, of necessity, been so restricted that only fragmentary plans have been recovered, allowing little to be deduced of the fourth century life style except that building techniques seem to have been maintained at a high level.

Fourth century Bath with its encircling defensive wall and network of approach roads imposed a structure on the landscape which succeeding generations were forced to acknowledge and adapt. The skeleton of the Roman settlement is still evident in the street plan of the city even today.

3. FROM PAGAN TO CHRISTIAN: THE SAXON REBIRTH

IN THE EARLY YEARS of the fifth century AD the centralized authority which had held the Roman Empire together for 500 years collapsed and Britain was left isolated to fend for itself in the face of the increasing numbers of Germanic migrants now arriving on the eastern and southern shores. The collapse meant that all the systems – economic, social and political – which had held the province together, fragmented. The manufacture of mass-produced goods such as pottery ceased, the supply of coinage stopped altogether and market centres wasted away. The Roman veneer was stripped off and what remained was essentially a Celtic tribal society in the process of being subsumed by the Germanic incursion.

On the western fringes of the country the arrival of the Saxon (Germanic) war leaders and their followers was delayed. Indeed, if we are to accept the traditional date of AD 577 – the year in which the *Anglo-Saxon Chronicle* tells us that the Battle of Dyrham was fought and the three cities of Gloucester, Cirencester and Bath passed into the hands of the Saxon leaders, Cuthwine and Ceawlin – then Bath survived in a sub-Roman twilight for more than a century and a half before the Saxon presence made itself felt. Five hundred years after Dyrham, in 1088, the same Chronicle records that Bath was ravaged in a rebellion led by Robert de Mobray against King William Rufus. By that stage, of course, Bath had for 22 years been under Norman rule but it was still, in physical form, essentially a Saxon town: its transformation was to follow a few years later.

Before we begin to consider how the town fared throughout the Saxon period it is necessary to say something about the evidence available to us. The documentary record is sparse. A few mentions in the *Anglo-Saxon Chronicle* together with a number of appearances in charters, mainly referring to land gifts to the Abbey, are all that we have. Taken together they provide very little insight into the nature of the settlement except to imply that its monastery was a flourishing concern. Archaeological excavation also has its limitations, the most serious being the fact that eighteenth and nineteenth century cellars have often totally removed the Saxon levels. Even so recent work  has discovered much that is new and unexpected. Some indication of Saxon life and style can also be gleaned from objects recovered from building works and excavations. In addition Saxon coins, from Bath and elsewhere, have allowed the history of the city's mint to be reconstructed, reflecting the

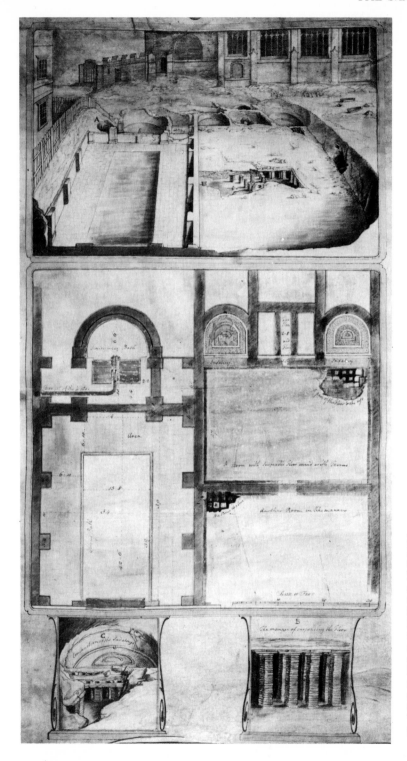

34. In 1755 Abbey House (the west range of the monastic claustral buildings) was demolished and during the excavation which followed part of the Roman bathing establishment was uncovered together with a number of graves belonging to the Saxon monastic cemetery. The original illustration by the famous Bath artist, William Hoare, details the discoveries.

growing importance of the place in late Saxon times. Finally there is the topography of the town as it has come down to us in later times: the line of the walls, the layout of the streets and gates, and the property boundaries of the major land holdings. It is surprising how much of what has survived to be recorded (and in many parts still survives) can be traced back to late Saxon times. Taken together all these disparate fragments can be used to sketch out a picture of the developing settlement during the period still generally referred to as the Dark Ages.

By the middle of the fourth century *Aquae Sulis* consisted of a group of magnificent Roman public buildings and private houses tightly packed within a defensive wall, while to the north, along the Fosse Way, and spreading out from it, was the depleted remnant of a once extensive unenclosed settlement, now encroached upon by cemeteries. It was a community in retreat, and the breakdown of the administrative and economic structure of the province sixty years later quickened the decline.

35.   The precinct of the Roman temple remained in use well into the sub-Roman period. Dirt and mud accumulated and from time to time a layer of rough cobbling was laid to consolidate the surface. The photograph shows the first of the cobble floors dating to the late fourth or early fifth century AD.

The collapse of civilized standards was vividly demonstrated in the excavation of the temple precinct (1979–84). Until some time after the middle of the fourth century the paving of the precinct was kept clean and in repair, even though some of the patches were rather rough and ready, but eventually the point had come when cleaning ceased, soil began to form, fragments of frost-shattered mortar and stone lay in the mud where they had fallen and the old precinct, now weed-grown and blowing with dead leaves, became a convenient tip for domestic refuse. Signs of decay were everywhere. Yet on at least five separate occasions the mire was consolidated with tips of rubble and sometimes with patches of rough paving using stones from the rapidly crumbling buildings (ill. 35). How long this process lasted it is impossible to say. It can hardly have been less than fifty years and was in all probability a good deal longer taking us well into the period of the sub-Roman twilight. The decay of the monuments is hardly surprising but what is particularly interesting is that consistent attempts were being made to maintain

36.   The excavation in the temple precinct showed that mud accumulation and cobble resurfacings built up the ground surface by half a metre before the massive blocks of the reservoir enclosure superstructure were thrown down. The section behind the horizontal rod shows the sequence of layers which developed on the old precinct floor in the 100–200 years after the precinct ceased to be properly cared for towards the end of the fourth century.

37. Many of the Roman buildings in the central area remained standing throughout the Saxon period though in ruins. Within and between them Saxon buildings were put up. The arrangement of the late Saxon street grid suggests that the old temple precinct wall may still have been preserved as a boundary. The position of the first Saxon abbey and of the church of St. Mary are not known for certain but fragments of masonry, which may belong to them, have been found and two Saxon cemeteries have been located. (Source: Cunliffe & Davenport 1985, fig. 105).

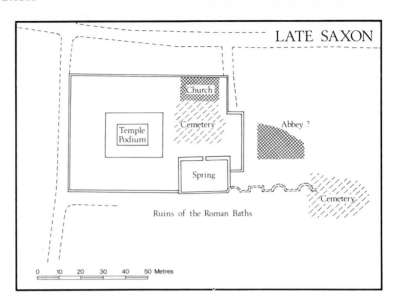

LATE SAXON

Church

Temple Podium

Cemetery

Abbey ?

Spring

Cemetery

Ruins of the Roman Baths

0   10   20   30   40   50 Metres

the area, if not as a religious precinct at least as a thoroughfare, over a considerable period of time. The latest substantial repaving incorporated slabs from the famous Gorgon's head pediment. It could, of course, be that they had simply fallen from the tottering four hundred year old building but another possibility is that they were deliberately pulled down and upturned in the mud to serve as paving by people, either pagans or Christians, who feared the ancient gods.

In considering the decay of Bath's great sanctuary buildings it would be wrong to think that all were reduced to a sea of rubble immediately after the breakdown of Roman order. Far from it. The structures themselves, by and large, stood for hundreds of years. Some of the more substantial were still there to dominate the scene in the eighth or ninth centuries to be wondered at, revered and even written about by people quite unable to practise the same building technology.

Elsewhere within the walled area there are hints of domestic building being used well into the fifth and possibly the sixth centuries. In Abbeygate Street excavations demonstrated a long sequence of occupation extending after the late fourth century. Towards the end a new masonry building, in a competent building style, was put up in the ruins of another. Still later an oven was inserted into one of its rooms and later still a severed human head found its way into the oven, indicating a certain lack of civilized standards. There is no way to date the sequence but it is a long one and the head could well have been of one of Bath's sixth century inhabitants.

Another site, in the western part of the walled area, close to Westgate Buildings produced traces of timber buildings with clay floors following a succession of Roman masonry structures, but again they are without firm dates.

In both instances these sub-Roman phases show that people were still living and working within the walled area of *Aquae Sulis* well into the fifth or even sixth century, perhaps even as late as the Battle of Dyrham in *c.* 577, but both successions end with abandonment followed by the accumulation of a thick black sterile soil. The impression is of a diminishing population. By the time the Saxon war leaders and their followers had penetrated the Cotswolds *Aquae Sulis* would have been an enclosure of gaunt ruins inhabited by ghosts and scavenging dogs, perhaps with a few scattered families and their pigs and chickens scratching a living among the crumbling walls while the springs flowed unabated.

If a date is wanted for the emergence of Bath from the ruins of *Aquae Sulis* the year 675 will suffice for in that year, in a foundation charter dated 6 November, Osric, king of the Hwicce, a sub-kingdom of Mercia, made a grant of certain estates to the Abbess Berta to enable a convent of the Holy Virgins to be established at Bath: there is good reason to believe that the founding nuns came from one or more of the Frankish monasteries near Paris. A few years later, in 681, in a charter giving more land to the community, the name of the Abbess, Bernguida, is recorded. She is evidently English but her deputy, Folcburg, is a foreigner.

Presently available evidence does not allow the location of the seventh century establishment to be pinpointed but it is most likely to have been within the walls. At a number of sites in England, early ecclesiastical foundations made use of pre-existing Roman enclosures partly for protection but largely to give a kind of legitimacy to the community by linking it to a powerful symbol of the past. If it lay within the walls of *Aquae Sulis*, where better than close to the main spring where the later Abbey is known to have developed. But the problem is confused by the fact that there is no further mention of a nunnery and the next we hear of the city, in a charter of 757–8, is of a grant of land to the brothers in the monastic church of St. Peter (certainly the precursor of the present Abbey church). The most likely explanation for all this is that the original foundation was in fact a double house of nuns and monks and that the seventh century establishment is the same as that mentioned from the eighth century onwards, the sisters, by this time, having dispersed or died out. Even so there is still the slight possibility

38.   Page from the Exeter Book. The book was given by Leofric, the first bishop of Exeter, to the Cathedral Library in 1072. It was composed of 131 leaves copied by a scribe in the late tenth century. The poem known as 'The Ruin' was written on two leaves scarred by fire or rot. It is thought to have been composed in the eighth century.

that the early nunnery founded by Osric may have lain elsewhere, perhaps even outside the walls. It is a problem which future excavation could, in theory, resolve.

At any event, from the mid eighth century the monastery of St. Peter, close to the ancient sacred spring, rose in fame and fortune and at the Synod of Brentford, held in 781, it is described as 'most famous' – though this may have been an unmerited compliment. No trace of the building has yet come to light, nor is its location recorded, but bearing in mind what is known of the state of the temple and baths at this time and of the location of the Saxon cemeteries, then one possibility is that the Abbey occupied what had been the precinct of the tholos temple to the east of the main Temple of Sulis Minerva (ill. 37). The precinct would have provided a convenient and relatively uncluttered space once the tholos was cleared away and its component parts dumped in the east end of the ruined baths. The crucial area is now partly beneath the Victorian Pump Room extension and partly beneath the present Abbey church and therefore largely inaccessible to excavation, but when the Pump Room extension was being built last century an extensive concrete foundation was found which would appear to have been of post- Roman and pre-Norman date. Little more can be said of it until new excavations are undertaken.

The use of old Roman precincts as sites for Saxon churches is a widely recognized phenomenon, occurring in Britain for example at Lincoln and York. It is a reminder that space was difficult to find in the centres of old Roman settlements where ruined buildings were probably standing quite high. A vivid reminder of this is provided by an eighth century poem called 'The Ruin' which comes down to us in fragmentary form in a collection of manuscripts known as the Exeter Book (ill. 38). The poem describes the grandeur of a ruined Roman town using the visions of the decayed might of a past age as an analogy for the tenuous nature of the achievements of man when contrasted with the power of God. Although the Roman town is not named the circumstantial evidence is overwhelmingly in favour of it being Bath. A few extracts will suffice to give an impression of the power of the language.

'Wondrous is this masonry shattered by the Fates ... the buildings raised by giants are crumbling ... the roofs have collapsed ... the towers are in ruins ... and so these courts lie desolate and the structure of the dome with its red arches sheds its tiles. There stood courts of stone and a stream gushed forth in rippling floods of hot water. The wall enfolded within its bright bosom the whole place which contained the hot flood of the baths'.

The description fits very closely with what is now known to have been the state of the King's Bath spring at about this time with its high standing reservoir walls, roofed with a great vault built of tiles and red mortar, containing the flow of hot water. The poet's description is uncommonly accurate and one can only suppose that the man himself stood in the temple precinct and, overawed by what he saw, composed his brilliant and evocative elegy. It is even possible that he was a monk resident in the nearby Abbey.

About this time the deliberate demolition of the reservoir enclosure, and possibly also of the rest of the baths, began. Evidence from the recent excavation shows that the massive stone blocks of the cornice and architrave capping the north wall of the reservoir were thrown to the ground but not before the iron clamps set in lead, which held them together, had been removed, no doubt as valuable scrap for reuse (ill. 36). Once the large and unwieldy blocks had been tumbled off, the small square blocks of stone of the main walls would be exposed, providing a ready source of building stone for the Saxon masons during the long process of building, extending, and rebuilding which would have marked the evolution of the Saxon monastic establishment. In William of Malmesbury's later account, the tenth century ecclesiastical buildings are described as 'known to be of wondrous workmanship' – a reference, no doubt, to their well-built masonry – still a comparative rarity in Britain at the time.

The two factors which contributed to the re-emergence of Bath were its monastery and its location in relation to the political boundaries of Saxon England. Bath sat on a frontier between Mercia in the north and Wessex in the south and its increasing importance as a potential military base is shown when in 781 the monastery was transferred from the control of the Bishops of Worcester to the Mercian king, Offa. At the same time Offa acquired land on the south side of the Avon presumably to create a bridgehead. Henceforth Bath began to be visited by the Mercian royal household. In 796 King Ecgfrith issued a charter from 'that celebrated town which is called in Saxon tongue *œt Baðun*' and in 864 the last of the Mercian kings, Burhred, held a gemot (a council meeting) at Bath attended by his queen, bishops and nobles.

In the late ninth century the power of Mercia declined with the rise of Wessex which culminated with Alfred's victory over the Danish marauders in 878. It was soon after this that the kingdom of the Hwicce, a sub-kingdom of Mercia, came under the control of the kings of Wessex: henceforth Bath belonged to Wessex.

One of the early acts of the Wessex kings was to strengthen the old Roman defences of Bath and to assign a militia to man them. This was part of a country-wide policy of creating a ring of strongly defended sites around the kingdom – places where the rural population could find shelter and troops could amass if and when the Danes attacked. The strong points were listed in a document known as the Burghal Hidage drawn up in the reign of Edward the Elder, King Alfred's immediate successor. Each site was assigned a number of hides of land, each hide reflecting a militia of a certain strength. Knowing the length of defensive circuit which a man was supposed to defend it is possible to compute the approximate total length of the defences. Bath is

39.   At the beginning of the tenth century the king, Edward the Elder, established a mint in Bath. Coins continued to be minted in the city until the reign of Henry I. 1, Edward the Elder with the name of Bath BAD on the reverse; 2, King Edgar; 3, King Edward the Martyr. (Scale 2:1).

assessed at 1000 hides which would allow a garrison of a size adequate to defend a circuit of 1375 yards. That the actual circumference of the Roman wall is 1250 yards strongly suggests that it was the Roman wall that was now being brought back into commission.

It is quite probable that the wall, now nearly 600 years old, was in need of extensive repair and there is some evidence for this in the early topographical accounts of Bath written in the sixteenth and seventeenth centuries, which described a number of Roman sculptures and inscriptions built into the city wall. From what we know of the Roman wall it was originally built of small blocks of neatly coursed stonework. This implies that the larger sculptured blocks represent patches and localized rebuild-ings some time when there was still plenty of Roman building stone to be had, much of it, in fact, coming from Roman funerary monuments. The late Saxon reordering of the defences would provide a reasonable context for the patching. Some further support for this was provided by a recent exam-ination of the ditch in front of the north wall at Upper Borough Walls where it was possible to demonstrate a phase of redigging and revetment in the late Saxon period.

Throughout southern Britain the tenth century was a period of urban growth and monastic revival. Bath benefited and its position on the northern border of Wessex ensured its continued political importance. In 901 the Witan (or parliament) was held in Bath under King Edward the Elder and it was during his reign that Bath's first Saxon mint was established (ill. 39) – a reminder of the growing economic importance of the settlement – but there was nothing to compare with the great event staged there seventy years or so later when, on 11 May 973, Edgar was crowned king of England in the Abbey church in the presence of Dunstan, Archbishop of Canterbury and Oswald, Archbishop of York. The service used then for the first time is that upon which the present coronation service is based.

The choice of Bath for so prestigious an event was quite logical: its monastery was a fine one, an ancient foundation with an increasing reputation but more important than that was Bath's frontier position. It had been Mercian for several hundred years and now it lay in Wessex. To some extent then it was border territory – where better to hold the coronation of the first king of England?

The exact location of the tenth century monastery has not been precisely established but it must have been close to or even beneath its medieval and later successor. Part of its cemetery has, however, been recorded immediately to the south of the present Abbey church in the area above the east end of the Roman baths. When the old Abbey House, which occupied the site, was demolished in 1755 a number of burials were found dug into the Roman ruins and beneath the head of one of them was found a small hoard of mid-tenth century coins (ill. 34). Another burial was discovered in archaeological excavations in 1968. It was lined with charcoal – a practice quite widespread in the late Saxon period. The nineteenth century excavations in the area produced part of a late Saxon stone cross together with a lead disc or coffin plate which bore an inscription referring to 'Eadgyvu . . . a sister of the community' (ills. 40–41). While at first sight this looks like evidence for the burial ground of the early nunnery founded by Osric it is certain that the script is much later and we can only suppose that the body of the nun was reinterred in the late Saxon monastic cemetery, suitably identified, in a new coffin.

Another early burial ground was found just to the north of the King's Bath spring. While this may have belonged to the

40. In 1898 a lead disc was found in the vicinity of the Saxon cemetery to the south of the abbey. It comes from the burial of Eadgyvu a sister of the religious community. It may be that her grave had been disturbed in the Late Saxon period perhaps during building work and that her remains were reburied in a new coffin identified with the lead cross. Scale 1:1.

41.   Stone crosses of Late Saxon date were often elaborately decorated with carved interlace patterns. Several fragments have been found in Bath offering a reminder of the high quality of Saxon craftsmanship. Scale 1:5.

monastery it is equally possible that it served the nearby church, the precursor of the medieval church of St. Mary de Stalle. At any event the two late Saxon cemeteries define western and southern limits for the monastic site, focussing attention once more on the mysterious concrete foundation found in the precinct of the tholos.

Nothing is yet known for certain of the style and finish of the monastic buildings but two scraps of evidence may offer some indication. One is a small two-light window found in the general area in the nineteenth century. It is of late Saxon type and could possibly have been part of the monastery (ill. 42). The other is a wax seal which was used on a manuscript dating to 1159–75 (ill. 43). The matrix itself, from which the impression was made, is generally thought to be of tenth century date. If this dating is correct then the building it depicts – with three apses each decorated with fluting and pilasters – is most likely to be the east end of the Saxon Abbey church. These hints of the possible appearance of the late Saxon structure are tantalizingly inadequate. Only through further excavation will tangible new evidence be secured.

42. Practically nothing is known of the Saxon monastery except that it was of outstanding workmanship. This small two-light window found near the present abbey may be all that survives of the Late Saxon building.

43. Seal from a matrix thought to be of tenth century date. This seal is actually used on a document of the period 1159–75. The building represented, with its three apses ornmented with pilasters, is probably the east end of the monastic church. If the seal is Late Saxon then this is the only surviving representation of the building in which Edgar was crowned king of England. If however it is later (later eleventh century) then it will be the cathedral priory of John of Tours. Scale 1:1.

The new vitality which southern England enjoyed under Alfred and his successors encouraged the growth of towns and with this came a need for ordered planning. The normal pattern seems to have been to divide the enclosed area into a number of large rectangular blocks separated from each other by streets and alleys and then to divide the blocks into strips or burghage plots for individual ownership. This kind of planning could only be imposed where there were no major impediments such as pre-existing buildings. Once established these street patterns and even some of the minor property boundaries have tended to survive and in a number of southern English towns like Winchester, Chichester and Wareham the late Saxon pattern can still be made out quite clearly today, even though medieval modifications have caused some distortion.

Bath presents a particularly interesting case where, in spite of the dominance of natural features such as the springs, the extensive replanning of the south-east quadrant in the Norman period and the cutting of new streets in the eighteenth and nineteenth centuries, there is still much to be seen of the late Saxon town plan. We can strip away the post-medieval changes quite easily by referring to Speed's map of 1610 (ill. 78). Here is the town still very much in its medieval guise, but to get back

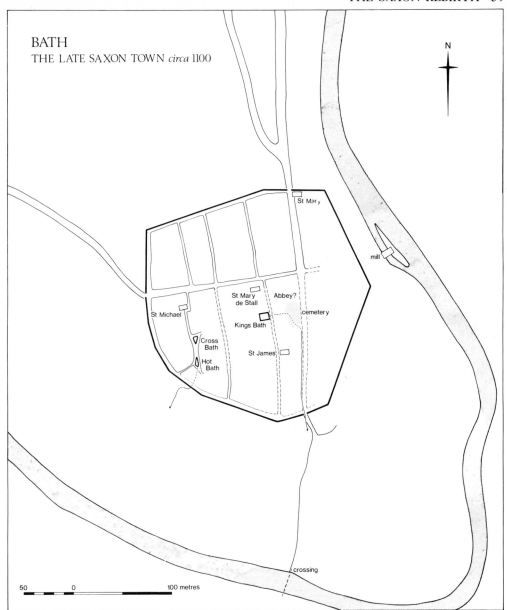

BATH
THE LATE SAXON TOWN *circa* 1100

N

St Mary

mill

St Mary
de Stall

Abbey?

St Michael

cemetery

Kings Bath

Cross
Bath

St James

Hot
Bath

crossing

50   0   100 metres

44.   In the tenth century the city wall of Bath was strengthened to make the settlement a defensible point during the uncertain period of Viking raids. It was probably at this time that the street grid was established and the land within was laid out in plots. Much of the Saxon street grid still survives in the modern street pattern. The south-east corner was, however, laid out afresh by the Normans to make space for the monastic precinct and there was another period of widening and realignment at the end of the eighteenth century. (Source: author).

to the pre-Norman situation requires a degree of controlled speculation. Nonetheless the attempt can be made with a certain degree of assurance (ill. 44).

The late Saxon plan was quite simple: the enclosed area was divided into two unequal parts by an east to west street, now Westgate Street and Cheap Street, and each half was divided into five elongated blocks by four north-south streets. The northern part still retains all four streets. Bridwell Lane, Parsonage Lane and Union Passage are still essentially the same narrow lanes they were in Saxon times but the fifth, High Street, was much widened in the medieval period (Union Street was cut much later as part of the great spate of improvements in the late eighteenth century). The street plan of the southern half is more difficult to reconstruct but two of the Saxon streets still survive in part, St. Michael's Place/Hot Bath Street, and Bimberry Lane, the northern continuation of which was largely removed during the eighteenth-century improvements. Of the two other suggested street lines in the south-east quadrant there is no trace, but this is entirely due to the total replanning of this area of the town in the late eleventh century as an extensive cathedral precinct. Stall Street, as we shall see, was part of that replanning. Yet there are still hints of the former lines to be found. The easternmost of the two missing streets, the southern continuation of High Street, is shown on the reconstructed plan passing through a gate in the wall. That gate was actually seen in a rescue excavation in 1951 (ill. 45). It had been blocked some time in the early medieval period and partially opened again in 1279 when it became known as Ham Gate. The outfall of hot water from the King's Bath was actually led along the line of the supposed street and out through a culvert beneath the gate to flow as an open leat to the river. A track led from the gate giving access to the meadow and probably to a southern crossing of the Avon. Taken together the evidence, though slight, supports the hypothesis of a continuous north-south street between a north and south gate.

The second of the missing north-south streets is less certain. The regularity of the plan certainly calls for it and there is one scrap of evidence in its support – the site of the preconquest church of St. James. A late Saxon church would be expected to be close to a street and the street-line suggested on the map would be in precisely the right position; it would also have provided access to the King's Bath spring.

The three springs of Bath would have imposed certain constraints upon the late Saxon street grid, requiring the planners to so arrange the streets that adequate access was provided together with a system of drains to remove the outfall. It is also quite probable that some of the Roman buildings were still sufficiently evident to impose themselves. This could well have been true of the Temple of Sulis Minerva, the outer precinct wall of which seems to have been respected by at least three streets (ill. 37), suggesting that the wall may still have been sufficiently high to have formed a boundary. Inside lay the spring, still within its reservoir enclosure, and the podium of the temple standing at or above Saxon ground level. Whether or not it was used as a building platform it is impossible to say. The front part of the old precinct was now a cemetery with the church of St. Mary tucked into the north-west corner quite possibly making use of the Roman precinct wall. Although our picture is very incomplete it does seem as though the skeleton of the Roman precinct was still making itself felt in the late Saxon period.

In the medieval period Bath had four parish churches within its walls all of which were probably of late Saxon origin. Two

THE HAM GATE

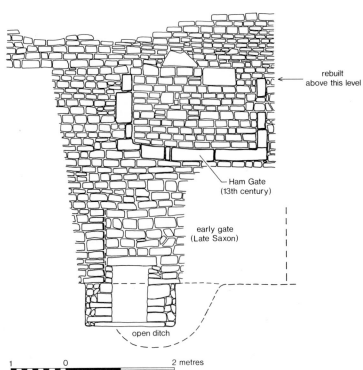

rebuilt
above this level

Ham Gate
(13th century)

early gate
(Late Saxon)

open ditch

1   0   2 metres

45. The site of Ham Gate was excavated in 1951. The earliest gate is most probably Late Saxon in origin and served as the original south gate of the city. When it was blocked in the early medieval period the open leet which flowed through it was canalized in a newly-built culvert. In the late thirteenth century a new opening was cut, after the ground level had risen considerably. It too was later blocked. (Source: author after Wedlake 1966).

have already been mentioned: St. James and St. Mary (later St. Mary de Stalle). The two others were St. Michael's in the western part of the town and St. Mary Northgate. St. Mary, as its designation implies, lay just inside the line of the town wall immediately adjacent to Northgate. This was a favourite position for late Saxon churches and can be paralleled, for example, at Wareham and at Oxford. So sited, the church could, if necessary, function as a strong point in times of attack, its tower providing a convenient look-out post.

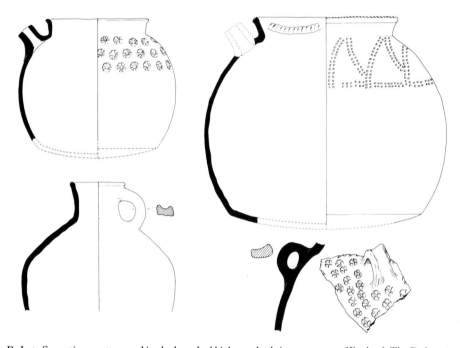

46.   By Late Saxon times pottery-making had reached high standards in many parts of England. The Bath region was well supplied with pitchers and cooking pots which were often highly decorated with impressed stamps. Scale 1:4. (Source: Cunliffe 1979, fig. 65).

By the tenth century, then, Bath had taken on the aspect of a small but prosperous town with four parish churches, three springs, a mint, and a monastery of national repute, all set within a regular grid of linking streets. The prestige of the monastic establishment was high and throughout the tenth century grants of land were being bestowed on it largely by the kings of Wessex. It was a time of religious revival and under the influence of Dunstan the community turned to the rule of St. Benedict. At the time of the Domesday survey the monastery held a manor within the city, a mill and 12 acres of meadow in the bend of the Avon.

A rough calculation, based on the number of burgesses recorded in the monastic manor and the number in the rest of the town suggests that the religious community covered about 13 per cent of the total walled area. Elsewhere the burgage plots laid out at the beginning of the tenth century were being taken up by artisans and merchants keen to move into such a rapidly developing centre. Although evidence of everyday life is sparse, sufficient archaeological material has been found to demonstrate the high technical quality of the pottery they used (ill. 46), which included finely-made green glazed jugs. One site in Westgate Buildings produced several spindle whorls and pin beaters, reminding us of the continuing importance of wool to the local economy. Safe behind the walls, in the shadow of a flourishing monastery, life must have been good.

The eleventh century was a time of turmoil and change: new forces were afield and they were soon to impinge on Bath. Renewed Viking attacks brought the Danish king Swein to Britain and after a successful summer campaign in 1013 he made for Bath where he received the formal submission of the western thegns (noblemen). There is no record of the inhabitants resisting – in all probability they did not – nor is there any archaeological trace of the event except possibly for a fine Viking sword found in the city ditch by Northgate (ill. 47).

The town will have continued little changed by the great events enacted a few years later on the fields of Hastings: for the average inhabitant of Bath the Norman Conquest meant little. But in the power struggle to follow Bath suffered. In 1088 the Norman bishops, led by Odo, rose in revolt in support of the king's brother, Robert of Normandy, and, using Bristol as a base, swept down on Bath and ravaged the town and the surrounding area. The particular attraction of Bath to the rebels lay in its strategic position and the fact that the king held substantial estates there.

No archaeological trace of the event has yet been found, nor was the extent of the damage recorded in contemporary accounts, but it must have been devastating for what was to follow was a complete reorganization. The revolt of 1088 marked the end of Saxon Bath and its Norman rebirth.

47. Recent rebuilding work on the site of the city ditch just outside north gate produced this fine Viking sword dating to the tenth century. The inlaid inscription was intended to read ULFBERHT ME FECIT (Ulfberht made me) but has been inaccurately copied. It was probably made in an Anglo-Scandinavian workshop in England. The scabbard was lined with fur to facilitate the drawing and return of the sword. (Scale 1:3)

4. MONKS AND WOOL: THE MEDIEVAL CITY

THE YEAR 1088 was a turning point in the history of Bath. William the Conqueror had died to be succeeded by his son William Rufus and in the inevitable uncertainty of such a transition a localized revolt had broken out during which Bath was attacked and, together with much of the surrounding countryside, was devastated by the rebels. But this was only one factor for in the higher echelons of the church there were also far-reaching changes in the air.

The conquest of England by William and his Norman knights, and the unashamed patronage which followed from it, created many anomalies in the ruling hierarchies which had, gradually, to be cleared up as the chance arose. In Bath, for example, the abbey seems, for some years, to have been ruled by two abbots. The more senior, Wulfwold, died about 1084 leaving his colleague Abbot Aelfsige in sole charge until he in turn died in 1087. The sack of Bath the next year and, coincidentally, the death of Bishop Giso of Wells, left William Rufus with a clean slate to reorganize as he wished. His solution was simple: in 1088 he appointed John of Tours, also called de Villula, Bishop of Wells. He was consecrated by Archbishop Lanfranc in July and at Lanfranc's suggestion the king made John a grant of the abbey of Bath together with all the property that went with it. It was a neat solution and one evidently to Bishop John's liking. He was a rich and intelligent man who clearly saw the advantages of Bath and as a skilled physician would no doubt have been fascinated by the potential of the curative springs. He was prepared to pay the king a considerable quantity of silver for the privilege, or, as a contemporary so delicately put it, 'to grease the king's hands with white ointment'.

Compared to the rustic dullness of Wells, Bath had particular attractions. Its abbey was famous, it was at a focal point of converging routes and its estates were rich. To a man of John's sophistication it was infinitely preferable to the obscurity of Wells. As soon as the grant of Bath abbey was confirmed in 1091, he removed the see of the Somerset bishopric from Wells to Bath, assuming at the same time the role of abbot. The result was that Wells was reduced to the level of a simple collegiate church, much to the annoyance of the clergy, while the monks of Bath became the bishop's chapter. Their church was now the mother church of the diocese and their resident head was a prior subordinate to the bishop.

The subsequent ecclesiastical history is complex and, mercifully, is not directly relevant to our theme. Suffice it to say that the twelfth and thirteenth centuries saw constant battles between the monks of Bath and the canons of Wells as to their relative powers and privileges. In 1159 the Pope, Adrian IV, had to intervene with a compromise judgment which included the injunction that the bishop was to be elected by representatives of the two chapters but in 1192 the monks of Bath elected a bishop without consulting Wells. The uproar and dissent which followed lasted until 1245 when Pope Innocent IV ordered that henceforth the bishop would be known as the Bishop of Bath and Wells and that this would be inscribed on the bishop's seal.

From the late twelfth century bishops had virtually abandoned Bath preferring to live at Wells but for a while they still retained the right to appoint the prior of Bath. In 1261, however, they returned the privilege to the monks, and though the bishop was still able to appoint other officials, he had become, by this stage, little more than the nominal head of Bath cathedral priory. It is against this background so briefly sketched that the fortunes of Bath can be assessed.

John of Tours was a man of energy and foresight with a strong sense of purpose. It was Bath that attracted him and it was here that he decided to create an establishment worthy of his aspirations. If it meant riding roughshod over the monks, it was no matter; anyway he considered them to be ill-educated ruffians – the attitude which many an arrogant Norman took with his Anglo-Saxon underlings. At the outset, therefore, he thought nothing of appropriating the dues and revenues of the monastic estates for his own purposes (though under the pressure of criticism he returned much in his later years).

Within the walled area of the city the church of Bath must have held about 3 acres of the total enclosed area of 24 acres much of the rest belonging to the king. This was clearly not enough for John's grandiose schemes. To lay out a monastery of the scale even approaching that he had been used to in his native Tours he needed far more land. The ravaged town following the rebel attack in 1088 cannot have been a particularly attractive property to its owner William Rufus and so in 1091 a deal was struck in which the king assigned his rights and properties in Bath to Bishop John. But these were uncertain times and ten years later, when a new king, Henry I, came to the throne, John was careful to reconfirm the deal sealing the bargain with a gift of 500 pounds of silver.

The scene was now set for John to bring his schemes to fruition. The great cathedral church, 90 ft. wide and more than 350 ft. long, was enormous by contemporary English standards. It must have been started in or soon after 1091 and at the time of

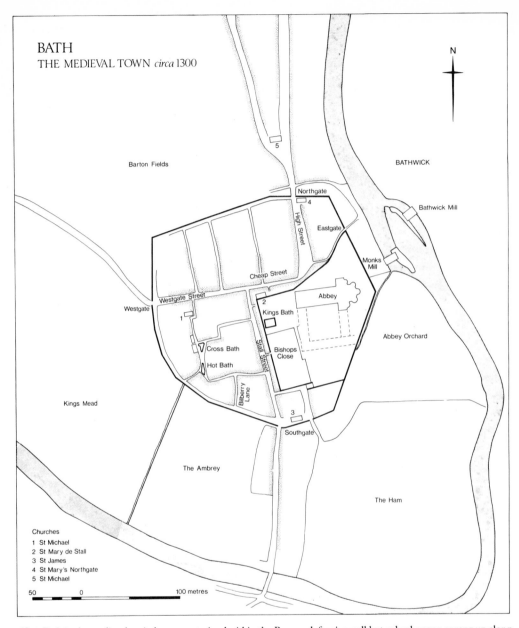

BATH
THE MEDIEVAL TOWN *circa* 1300

N

Barton Fields

BATHWICK

Northgate

Bathwick Mill

High Street

Eastgate

Cheap Street

Monks Mill

Westgate Street

Abbey

Westgate

Kings Bath

1

2

Cross Bath

Bishops Close

Stall Street

Abbey Orchard

Hot Bath

Kings Mead

Bilberry Lane

3

Southgate

The Ambrey

The Ham

Churches
1 St Michael
2 St Mary de Stall
3 St James
4 St Mary's Northgate
5 St Michael

50   0   100 metres

48.   Bath in the medieval period was constrained within the Roman defensive wall but suburbs soon sprang up along the roads leading to the north and south gates. Inside the walls the Saxon street grid continued to dominate the city except in the south-east corner where a new precinct was created to contain the monastic establishment and the Bishop's Palace. Stall Street was laid out at this time to replace one or more Saxon streets obliterated by the new precinct. The four churches within the walls were probably of Late Saxon origin. One of these, St. James, came within the new monastic precinct and was used by the Bishop. A replacement was built by the south gate in 1279. The church of St. Michaels outside the north gate was probably newly constructed in the medieval period to serve the growing northern suburb. (Source: author).

John's death in December 1122 it was by no means complete. A contemporary account says that the church had been finished 'up to the lower vaultings' suggesting that the great nave was still unroofed though it, and other unfinished parts, were probably given temporary roofing of timber and the claustral buildings may also have been temporary wooden structures. So much timber would explain the ease with which the buildings burnt first in 1117 and more seriously in July 1137 during the anarchy. A new building programme was instigated by Bishop Robert of Lewes who had been appointed by King Stephen the previous year. Bishop Robert was an enthusiastic builder at Bath and during his thirty-year reign (1136–1166) he erected a chapter house, cloister, refectory, infirmary and other conventual buildings. In other words he seems to have finished off the building programme which John of Tours had begun. If this is so, to have completed the monastic complex in 70 years was no mean achievement. The only significant alteration to be made after this was the construction of a lady chapel by Bishop Bytton (1267–74).

Perhaps one of the most surprising aspects of Bath is that there is virtually nothing of the great eleventh century monastery now to be seen, except for a few fragments if the visitor knows exactly where to look, but fossilized in the plan of the city, in its street lines and property boundaries, the ghost of the monastic precinct is there to be traced. To this, archaeological activity has, over the years, added a wealth of detail with the result that it is now possible to see how Bishop John set about redesigning the city: the charred ruin he inherited was transformed into a place of wonder.

First and foremost he needed space, but this was no problem for he had acquired most of the city from the king and therefore had a free hand to design as he wished. What happened can best be judged by comparing the two maps (ills. 44 and 48). In short John carved out an extensive new precinct occupying a quarter of the walled area of the town and in doing so destroyed two of the southern streets almost entirely, enclosing within the precinct the old late Saxon abbey of St. Peter, the church of St. James and the King's Bath spring.

The dislocation of the old street grid was considerable. The main east-west street was truncated at the junction with High Street (the East gate and the alley leading to it are probably later), while a totally new street, Stall Street, was laid out, just outside the western boundary of the precinct, running southwards to a new South gate. It was probably at this time that the late Saxon South gate was blocked after the open leat

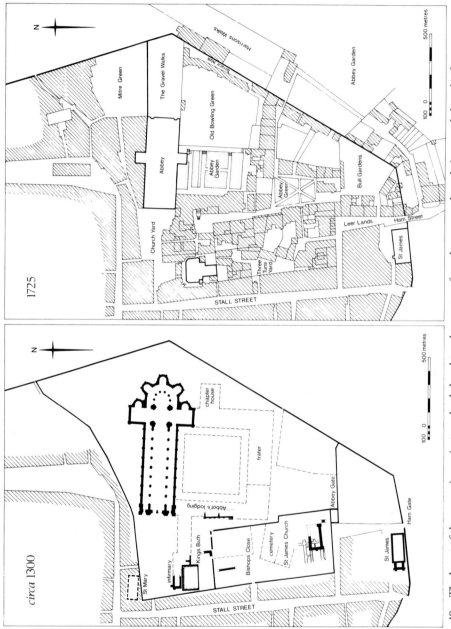

49.   The layout of the monastic precinct can be deduced to a large extent from the property boundaries recorded on the first accurate large-scale map of Bath in 1725. The abbey lay above the nave of the Norman cathedral priory church parts of which have been found in excavation. From this, the plan of the establishment can be outlined. The Bishop's Close lay in the south-west corner with its own gate to Stall Street. The skewed boundaries within probably delineate the original Saxon church of St. James: part of its cemetery was found recently. A small fragment of the precinct wall, just east of abbey gate, still survives. (Source: author).

running through it and taking the outflow from the King's Bath spring, had been canalized in a stone-built culvert (ill. 45).

The precinct was defined, so William of Malmesbury tells us, 'with a great and elaborate circuit of walls', built, no doubt, of stone robbed from old Roman buildings. The main gate lay towards the south-west corner, its site still perpetuated in the street name – Abbeygate Street. Another gate, due east of it, known as Lodgate, gave access through the city wall to Abbey Orchard which lay between the town and the Avon, and the Saxon church of St. Mary at the north-western corner may have commanded an approach from Stall Street or Cheap Street giving direct to the east front of the cathedral priory church.

Apart from the King's Bath spring and the Saxon church of St. James, John had a free hand with the internal layout of his new establishment (ill. 49). The Saxon monastic church of St. Peter was pulled down and in its place was constructed the new cathedral priory church, among the largest Norman churches in Britain. To the south of it land was set aside for the great cloister and the surrounding claustral buildings. Some of them may even have been erected in temporary materials, but it was left to Bishop Robert to replace them in stone in the middle of the twelfth century.

The whole of the south-west corner of the precinct was occupied by the Bishop's Close where the Bishop's Palace lay. The boundaries of the close were still evident as late as the early eighteenth century. Within, boundary lines askew to the principal axis may be those of the late Saxon church of St. James which was encapsulated within the close and used as a private chapel by the bishops. The situation was clearly unsatisfactory and in 1279 Bishop Robert of Bath and Wells granted two closes of land to the Prior and Convent of Bath so that in one of them 'within the city wall from the south gate of the city to the close of the priory they shall construct a parish church of St. James in lieu of the church of St. James adjoining the Bishop's chamber, the chancel of which the Bishop has thought fit to remove reserving for himself and his successors the nave or body of the church as a site for a chapel'. In other words by the late thirteenth century the bishops were feeling guilty of having appropriated for their own use one of the town's few late Saxon churches and had given land near the South gate so that a replacement could be built.

Once the cathedral priory and the Bishop's Close have been accounted for, there is very little room left within the precinct boundary. In the south-east corner there seems to have been an open area probably a garden the shrunken remains of which are

still represented by the delightful calm of Abbey Green. The north-east corner, north of the church, was probably the monastic cemetery. This leaves the north-west corner in front of the west door of the church, which was occupied by the King's Bath, and a range of claustral buildings. In spite of John's desire to create a large and imposing precinct the sheer scale and complexity of his individual buildings must have left it with a decidedly built-up feeling.

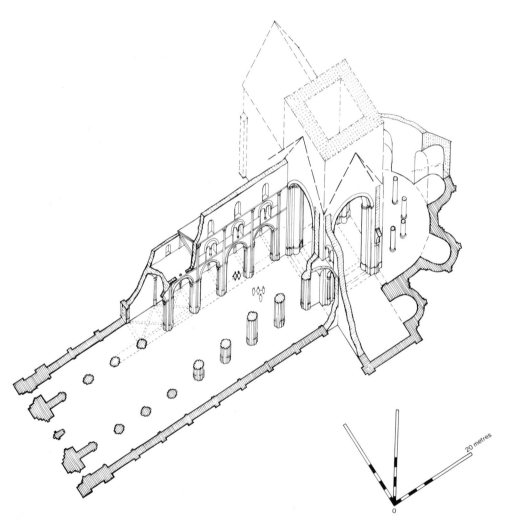

50. The ground plan of the Norman church can be restored using the evidence recorded by James Irvine together with the results of recent excavations beneath Orange Grove. Some scraps of Norman superstructure survive built into the east end of the later abbey. Taken together this evidence allows the form of John of Tours' great church to be appreciated, if only in outline. (Source: Sheila Gibson).

Of the great Norman church very little now remains: it was virtually destroyed to make way for the present abbey church built in the early sixteenth century over the nave of its Norman predecessor (ills. 49 and 50). The original building was of the same width but was considerably longer. Some scraps, however, survive. A Norman arch and other mutilated detail remain high up in what is now the east wall of the south aisle choir and while alterations were being made between 1863 and 1872, involving extensive refloorings, the Clerk of Works, James Irvine, recorded details of pier bases and of the west front. To this may be added the plan of one of the apsidal chapels attached to the east end, located in an archaeological excavation in 1979 incongruously sited beneath what is now the Orange Grove traffic island. Taken together it is evident that Bishop John's church must have been at least 350 ft. long: it was of aisled cruciform plan with an apsidal east end enlivened by three radiating chapels.

This kind of arrangement in which the east end, or presbytery, was apsidal with the aisles carried around the apse as an ambulatory (a processional way) was a typically Norman plan which had limited popularity in Britain, though examples can be found at Norwich, St. Augustine's, Canterbury, Westminster Abbey and Bury St. Edmunds. It was however the kind of building which would have been very familiar to John in his northern French homeland and reflected his taste for the Norman French culture he had left behind.

John was evidently intent on making Bath a convent of international reputation. He was not impressed by the resident monks, regarding them as stupid barbarians and he treated them quite harshly, but gradually he introduced a new breed of more educated men. As William of Malmesbury tells us, he 'completed many things nobly in ornaments and books, and filled the abbey with monks eminent for literature and discharge of their duties. According to report, his medical knowledge was founded more upon practice than science. He enjoyed literary society but indulged in sarcasm more than was fitted to his rank. He was a wealthy man and of liberal habits, but could not be induced, even on his death-bed, wholly to restore their lands to the monks'. It is a particularly penetrating pen-portrait giving a distant taste of what life must have been like in the close-knit religious community under John's arrogant rule.

Bath's most famous scholar monk was Adelard. He had spent some time among the Saracens of Italy and Apulia learning Greek and Arabic philosophy and science, and will have

returned to Bath bringing with him a range of knowledge that was both novel and dangerously exciting to his local audience. It was in this way, in the great religious houses, that medical science developed, rooted deep in the writings of the early Arabic scientists that were only now becoming known in the west.

John's interests in medicine and science must have been one of the reasons why he found Bath, with its natural thermal springs, so attractive and it was most probably under his reign that the King's Bath was renovated. The earliest reference to the medical baths is a document known as the *Gesta Stephani* (the Works of King Stephen) compiled about 1138. The writer states that, 'Through hidden channels are thrown up streamlets of water, warmed without human agency, and from the very bowels of the earth, into a receptacle beautifully constructed with chambered arches. These form baths in the middle of the city, warm and wholesome and charming to the eye'. He goes on, 'Sick persons from all England resort thither to bathe in these healing waters, and the strong also, to see these wonderful burstings out of warm water and to bathe in them'.

The Norman builders would have found the Roman reservoir enclosure still very much in evidence (ill. 51). The great vault

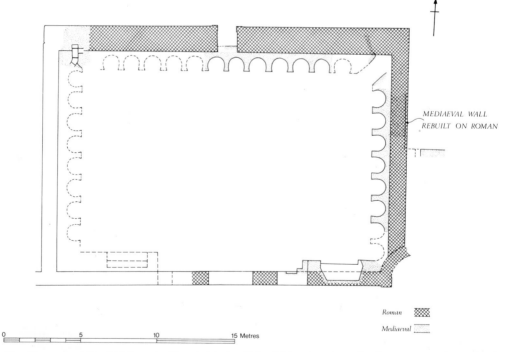

MEDIAEVAL WALL
REBUILT ON ROMAN

Roman
Mediaeval

0   5   10   15 Metres

51.   The medieval King's Bath survived largely intact until the eighteenth century when improvements obscured and destroyed much of the original structure.

had long since fallen and the walls themselves had been used as a convenient source of building stone for hundreds of years. But the stump of the west, north and east walls was still standing above the contemporary ground level, while the south wall with its three great Roman arches was substantially intact. Within the enclosure the old reservoir was now full of sand and rubble so the water-level would have been higher than in Roman times, the water lapping the reservoir enclosure walls. The Norman builders, then, were confronted with a rectangular pool surrounded by a thick wall and with a solid floor of sand and rubble.

There is now sufficient evidence from the recent programme of excavations to show that a series of arched semi-circular recesses were constructed against the inside of the west, north and east walls – the 'chambered arches' of the *Gesta Stephani* – with two stairways, or slips leading down into the water at the north-west and north-east corners. The stumps of the Roman walls were heightened with new masonry to the level needed to support the upper part of the arches and any balustrading that might have adorned the enclosure. This basic arrangement, created in the early twelfth century, was to remain, virtually

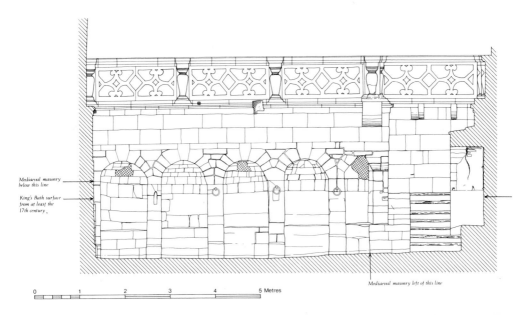

Mediaeval masonry below this line

King's Bath surface from at least the 17th century.

Mediaeval masonry left of this line

0   1   2   3   4   5 Metres

52. Recent work has exposed the foundation of the north wall of the King's Bath while the east wall (shown here in elevation), still substantially medieval, was re-exposed a hundred years ago. Johnson's view of the King's Bath in 1675 (below ill. 72) shows what is essentially the medieval structure in active use. (Source: Cunliffe & Davenport 1985, figs. 49 and 50).

untouched, until the late seventeenth century and can be very clearly seen in Thomas Johnson's drawing of 1675 (ill. 72). Eighteenth and nineteenth century 'improvements' have destroyed or obscured much of the Norman work but the lower parts of several of the northern recesses were seen beneath what is now the viewing corridor between the spring and the temple precinct, while four recesses, their upper parts later rebuilt, are still to be seen along the east wall of the King's Bath.

What is a little surprising about all this is the very early date at which the spring was converted into a well-appointed bath of some elegance. Its considerable size may have been dictated by the existing Roman structures but it is clear from the description in the *Gesta Stephani* that the bath was already widely known and frequented. How much of this was due to a reawakening occasioned by John of Tours' energies and how much to long established traditions it is impossible to say.

There were two other baths within the monastic precinct. The early sixteenth century topographer John Leland, having described the King's Bath, notes that 'Ther goith a sluse out of this Bath, and served in Tymes past with Water derived out of it 2 Places in Bath Priorie usid for Bathes: els voide; for in them be no springes'. According to later writers these two baths were known as the Abbot's and the Prior's Baths and must have lain somewhere to the east of the King's Bath. A map of the city, drawn by William Smith in 1588, well after the dissolution of the priory, does, in fact, show a pool, identified as the Mill Bath, in just such a position (ill. 53) and it was here later, making use of the same source, that the Duke of Kingston built his baths in 1755.

In 1867 James Irvine, Clerk of Works at Bath abbey, was able to record a substantial length of fine Norman masonry, with shallow buttresses along its length and a clasping corner buttress, south of the west end of the abbey in the vicinity of which were several contemporary drains. Stylistically the building must be early Norman and is aligned with the axis of the King's Bath. The implication would seem to be that the buttressed wall was part of the Prior's Bath and that it was probably laid out at the beginning of the twelfth century when the King's Bath was built. One point of particular interest is that the two baths were set askew to the axis of the church as though they were regarded as two separate building complexes. This would have posed no problems all the time that the cloisters and conventual buildings were unstarted (or were represented only by temporary structures), but when Bishop Robert of Lewes began his building programme to complete the monastery his

west range would have had to incorporate the Prior's Bath, and no doubt the Prior's Lodgings which was part of it, in spite of its eccentric angle. This may explain why the final version of this range, which survived as Abbey House until 1755, was of such an irregular plan.

We have skated over the problem of the Abbot's Bath which appears to have been separate from the Prior's Bath: indeed Leland specifically mentions two baths. If this were so, the simplest explanation would be to suppose that they were both housed in the same building, but there is no proof of this.

Of the claustral buildings, erected in the middle of the twelfth century, virtually nothing is known. The plan of the cathedral priory at Bath would, however, have been broadly similar to the other Benedictine houses of England. The east range, continuous with the south transept of the church, would have housed the chapter house where the convent assembled for meetings, and probably also the dorter range wherein lay the monks' sleeping accommodation. The site of the range is now entirely built over but must have run north-south across what is now the eastern end of York Street. On the southern side of the cloister would have been the frater or the dining hall of the

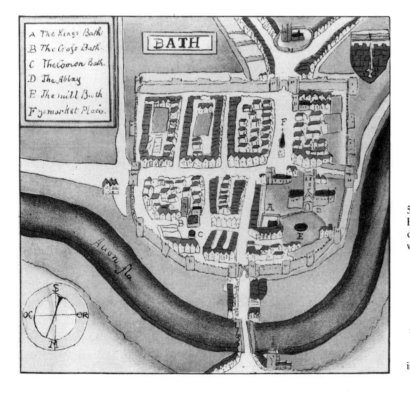

53. The earliest map of Bath, by William Smith, dates to 1588. Although very schematic, it gives a good idea of the open precinct soon after the Reformation before building had begun to encroach upon it. The Mill Bath shown just south of the abbey may be the remnants of the Prior's Bath mentioned in medieval manuscripts.

monks with a separate kitchen nearby. In terms of the modern
city plan this would have occupied the area running from the
north side of Abbey Green, along the northern side of Lilliput
Lane. The west range, as we have said, was probably wholly
occupied by the Prior's Lodgings and guest accommodation, the
only part of the monastery to survive the dissolution to become
Abbey House.

The only other major building to locate is the infirmary. This
probably occupied the area between the west range and the
King's Bath and part of it may have extended along the north
side of the King's Bath where the foundations of a massive
buttressed building of mid-twelfth century date were discovered
during recent excavations beneath the Pump Room. A position
close to the curative waters of the bath would be a sensible one
to choose for such a building.

In spite of its architectural pretentions the monastic establishment was never very crowded. Even at its most flourishing at
the beginning of the thirteenth century there were never more
than about 40 monks in residence and from then on the number
gradually declined until 1344 when the Black Death devastated
the town, reducing the convent to about 20. Thereafter the
number remained more or less constant until the dissolution.

The other major element of the religious establishment was
the Bishop's Palace which Leland, writing in the early sixteenth
century, tells us lay in the south-western part of the precinct.
Little remained in his time, with the exception of a ruined tower,
but the boundaries of the Bishop's Close were perpetuated in
subsequent land divisions and were finally planned with some
degree of accuracy in an estate map produced for the Duke of
Kingston in 1725 (ill. 49). Most of the boundaries recorded
within the close were parallel or at right angles to the major land
divisions, representing the close walls, and are thus likely to
reflect the positions of the buildings constituting the Bishop's
Palace, but one set of boundaries are entirely askew. These can
hardly be other than the limits of the churchyard of the late
Saxon church of St. James which was incorporated into the new
palace close. In 1279, as we have seen, it was partly demolished,
the rest serving as a private chapel for the bishop. Part of the
cemetery, presumably of late Saxon date, was located in a trial
excavation but no trace of the church has yet been seen.

In 1984–5 it was necessary to carry out a rescue excavation in
the south part of the Bishop's Close on a plot of land in the
angle of Swallow Street and Abbeygate Street which was about
to be developed for new shops. What emerged was a substantial
part of the Bishop's Palace complex (ill. 54). The earliest

54.   The medieval Bishop's Palace was a complex structure frequently improved and rebuilt. The photograph of the excavation of 1984 shows the north-west corner of the early twelfth century hall with a later twelfth century wall abutting the corner (at the top left). A series of thirteenth century additions can be seen top right. The square tank is eighteenth century.

building, dating to *c.* 1100 was a typical Norman upper-halled house 18.4 m long by 9.6 m wide, with traces of clasping buttresses at the corners. These buildings, as the name implies, consisted of a main hall at first floor level, reached by a flight of external stairs, above a vaulted cellar or undercroft which could often only be entered from the hall above. The emphasis was on security. Some time in the twelfth century the hall was extended westwards and there is some evidence of the extension having incorporated a tower. These were troubled times – times of civil war and anarchy – when prudent bishops elsewhere in the country were busy fortifying their palaces: Bath seems to have been no exception.   The complex remained unchanged for some time until the thirteenth century when much of the old hall was destroyed, the remnants being incorporated in a building of totally different plan with thinner walls enlivened by deep buttresses. The rebuilding could be a reflection of a more significant change coming about in Bath in the middle of the thirteenth century. The bishops, now of Bath and Wells, had grown tired of Bath and favoured Wells for their permanent residence, though as we have seen there were still changes being made towards the end of the century when St. James' church

was converted to a chapel. However, by 1328 Bishop Reginald dismissed the bishop's residence as ruinous, redundant and too expensive to maintain and was glad to make it over to the priory for an annual rent of twenty shillings.

Another discovery of some interest in this area was of a well-built medieval drain running beneath Swallow Street. It is evidently the main outfall constructed by Bishop John to take the overflow from the King's Bath and probably linked up with the culvert found passing through the city wall at the site of Ham gate.

Taken together the results of this limited rescue excavation show how much there is to learn of the medieval city, and in particular the Bishop's Palace if the chance of further work ever arises.

The discussion so far has concentrated largely upon the monastery and this is quite proper, for the bishop and the prior were men of substance in the medieval community whose power and influence pervaded every corner of the town. Nonetheless, outside the precinct boundary the city continued to develop and gradually civic institutions and secular interests began to stand up for themselves.

For much of the medieval period the core of the city lay within the walls which it was the city's responsibility to maintain in good order as a contribution to the defence of the realm. In 1275 Edward I issued a writ to empower a jury to be set up to investigate complaints that the monks were removing stones from the city wall to repair their mill, and when they met they uncovered positive evidence that this was so. There must always have been a temptation to use the city wall as a quarry and to a king conscious of the growing threat of France the weakening of urban defences must have been anathema.

The problem became of even more concern during the French wars which threatened throughout the fourteenth century. The town was granted exemption from murage in 1341, but in 1369–70 a further representation was made to the king that evil-doers were breaking down the wall and carting off stones. The king, Edward III, acknowledged the problem and empowered the mayor and his deputies to levy a contribution for the repair of the walls and towers on 'all owners of lands, tenements and rents within the city and suburbs, and all who constantly dwell therein, and resort thither for merchandise, and also to take as many carpenters, masons and other workmen as may be necessary, and set them upon the work at the expense of the commonality of the city'. In other words all those who benefited from the city had to contribute to the upkeep of the walls and it was the mayor's responsibility to see that they did. Much the same happened again seven years later under Richard II in 1377, when fear of French invasion was in the air, but thereafter, as foreign threats to the realm receded, so the walls were left untended to crumble slowly, helped in their decay by those searching for the occasional supply of building materials.

The circuit of the walls, whatever its state of readiness to face attack, constrained the city. Two of the old Saxon gates (probably Roman in origin) continued in use: the West gate and the North gate. To these were added a South gate at the end of the newly-created Stall Street, replacing the old South gate to the east. Somewhat later, perhaps as late as the fourteenth century, a small and unobtrusive East gate was built, linked by a

55. The medieval east gate of the city is the only gate still to survive. It was a minor gate providing access from the centre of the town to the river's edge where a ferry crossed to Bathwick and where the mills lay. The gate can still be seen, largely beneath recent buildings. In this photograph taken in 1900 before the Empire Hotel was completed part of the city wall with battlements still survives.

lane to the main street grid, and giving access to a way down to the ferry across the river (ill. 55). At a later date this path was called Boat Stall Lane. The North, South and West gates were all demolished in the late eighteenth century to make way for improved communications and are recorded only in schematic form on Speed's map of 1610, and the 'Frenchman's plan' of 1650 (ill. 50) but the diminutive East gate, overtaken by developments, was left untouched and, remarkably, still survives.

Within the confines of the wall and constrained by the late Saxon street grid the town developed. In the south-west corner the two springs – the Cross Bath and the Hot Bath – were probably fitted out with arched recesses in the same manner as the King's Bath. It was in this form that they survived to be recorded by Leland in the early years of the sixteenth century, and close by was the Hospital of St. John the Baptist, occupying the plot between the two baths and the west wall of the town.

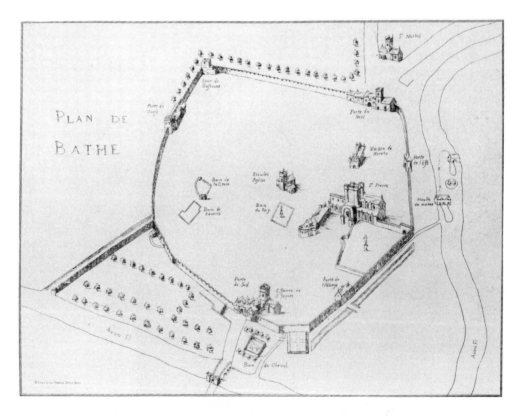

56. This anonymous map of Bath, now in the British Museum, was produced by a Frenchman in c 1650. It shows the walls and churches of the medieval city in convincing detail.

The hospital was founded in 1174 by Bishop Reginald Fitz Josceline as a charity to look after poor people who had recourse to visit the neighbouring baths. Provision was made to accommodate 6–8 almsfolk who were distinguished by their blue gowns and were accordingly known as the 'Blue Alms'. It was in this way that medieval society cared for those in need. Another almshouse – the Hospital of St. Catherine – was founded nearby, in Bynbury Lane in 1444, by William Phelippes, mayor of Bath in 1432. It comprised four almshouses providing accommodation for eight people. The establishment remained on its original site until 1825, when redevelopment and the construction of the former Royal United Hospital displaced it to a site near the Beau Street swimming baths. Here, in mock Tudor pastiche, the hospital remains today.

Besides the two almshouses the walled core of the city could boast four parish churches: St. James near the South gate, established there in 1279, and the three ancient late Saxon churches of St. Mary de Stalle, St. Michael and St. Mary North gate. Very little is known about their physical forms except the crude pictorial representations which appear on Speed's map and the Frenchman's Map, but all four appear to have had western towers. Of these the most important was St. Mary de Stalle. It was the official church of the city and had a chantry chapel dedicated to St. Catherine, patron saint of Bath, where the Freemen of Bath would gather to admit new members. One of the aisles was set aside for the Mayor and Corporation. In many ways St. Mary's was the symbol of the city, standing boldly against the great priory church only a few steps from it. Inevitably there were conflicts and matters came to a head in 1421. The monks argued that, by custom, none of the city churches should ring their bells in the morning before the abbey bells had rung, nor after curfew. An inquisition was held and inevitably a compromise was reached, but the issue is interesting in showing the city flexing its muscles against the stranglehold of the priory.

Churches, baths and hospitals together did not take up too much of the space within the restricted, if adequate, street grid. Elsewhere along the frontages, set within burgage plots established in the tenth century, were the houses of the merchants, craftsmen and labourers. For the most part they would have been timber structures with thatched roofs, though some, the more wealthy, were built in masonry. Away from the frontages the spacious garden areas were used for the digging of rubbish pits, found in great number wherever excavation is possible. No doubt much of the domestic rubbish was disposed of in this way,

but in common with the practices of the time sewage tended to be dumped over the city walls, or worse, thrown into the streets to clog and foul the open culverts of water that ran through most of the public ways. It was not until the sixteenth century that these traditional practices were brought to an end and a town scavenger was appointed whose job it was to collect the city's waste and to cart it out through the West or South gates to be dumped in the mixens (or rubbish heaps) round about. Nowadays any excavation in the area usually exposes a thick layer of black soil, sterilized by age but nonetheless a reminder that the approach to the city in medieval times might not have been an altogether pleasant experience. The low-lying and often airless condition of Bath would have heightened the experience.

57. St. Michaels, in the northern suburb, was a medieval church seen here in a lithograph of *c* 1835. The old medieval building with its renaissance porch was pulled down in 1731 and replaced by a more grand building in classical style.

Perhaps it was with this partly in mind that a Frenchman, writing to a youth about to visit the city in the fourteenth century, could advise 'Bath, situated, or rather buried, in deep valleys in the middle of a thick atmosphere and a sulphureous fog, is at the gates of Hell'.

The heart of every medieval town was its market and Bath was no exception. Here the essential open space was created by widening the late Saxon street leading southwards from the North gate, to provide room for the local traders to put up their temporary stalls and pen their animals on the weekly market day. The width of the market place has become fossilized in street frontages which today give Northgate Street its spacious proportions.

As the prosperity of the city increased so extramural development became inevitable. The earliest suburb developed close to the old market area, just outside North gate where Broad Street and Walcot Street converge, creating a wide triangular space which would have allowed a northwards extension of the market. Set back at the base of the triangle and facing North gate was the church of St. Michael extra Northgate (ill. 57). The earliest reference to the church is in a priory cartulary of the early thirteenth century, so it is most likely to be a late eleventh or twelfth century foundation created to serve the need of the extramural population.

The north suburb has a very deliberate planned look about it. This is apparent on Gilmore's map (ill. 59) where large plots of even size are indicated running from Walcot Street down to the river and also westwards from Broad Street. A number of mid-thirteenth century deeds refer to these strips being rented or purchased and some imply that they were being farmed by their urban holders involving them in some of the responsibilities and services of land-holding. In other words they began as extra mural allotments but gradually houses were built on them and a resident population developed. An interesting insight into this process is provided by a deed in which Jordan Smith granted his son Adam the land which he had acquired outside North gate and in return Adam had to provide his father with all the necessities of life. This looks very much like a stage in the colonization of the suburb in which previously open land was being settled and worked by the younger generation. The ordered layout of much of the northern suburb was very probably a deliberate act of land allotment, the most likely context for which was the great reorganization of the city by John of Tours about 1100. John's plans for the cathedral priory had required the appropriation of considerable areas of

land within the city walls. It could well be that the dislocated population was now settled in the newly-created suburbs north and south of the city or at least given land there in compensation.

Such an important suburb was bound to be provided with some form of river crossing – the precursor to the much later Pulteney Bridge. We have already suggested that a Roman crossing may have existed at this point: its medieval successor is indicated by the narrow lane, known as Alford Lane, which led from the area in front of North gate down to the river where presumably an ancient ford persisted. (The lane still, in part, survives.) By the seventeenth century, as Speed's map indicates, the ford had been replaced by a ferry guided by an overhead rope.

John of Tours' great replanning of Bath created a new South gate from which a new street – now Southgate Street – led down to the southern crossing of the Avon. Here again there are distinct traces of a regularly laid out suburb with elongated plots extending back from the street (ill. 58). Beyond these to the east and the west were the town marshes and meadows, known as the Hams, where the urban rubbish was tipped. The western meadow was limited on the west by a substantial boundary, part wall and part fence, which ran from the south-west corner of the

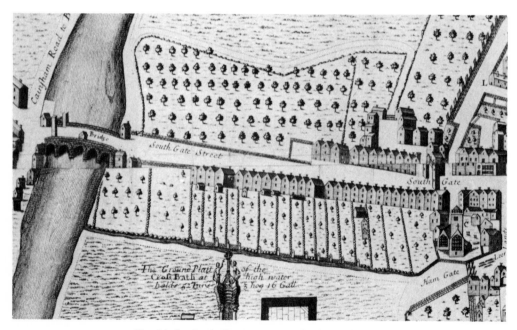

58. Medieval suburbs grew up outside the north and south gates.

city wall to the river. It could well have originated as a defensive
work protecting the southern approaches to the city, but its date
of construction is unknown.

Southgate Street led to the city bridge, which was certainly in
existence in the medieval period and in all probability was built
by John of Tours who would frequently have used this southern
approach en route to and from Wells. The best impression of
the elegant structure is given by Bernard Lens' drawing dated
1718 (ill. 61) which shows the five broad arches on which the
road was taken together with the tower-like gate at its southern
end. The little building in the centre was an oratory dedicated to
St. Lawrence where travellers might make offerings in thanks
for, or the expectation of, a safe journey.

Further afield, at the approaches to the medieval town, were
several ecclesiastical establishments administered by the abbey.

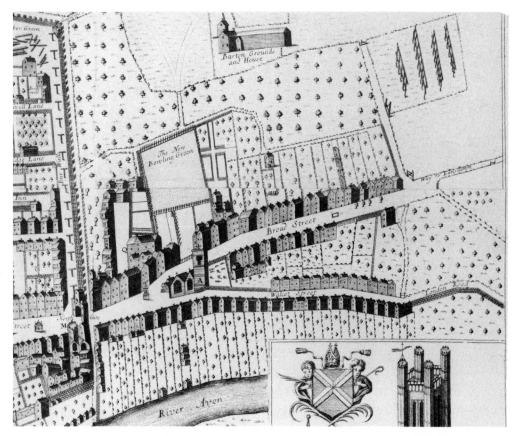

59.   The north suburb was of considerable size: it had its own church, St. Michaels and an adjacent wide street
which could be used as an extension to the High Street Market.

To the north, at the top of Broad Street (now Fountains Buildings at the bottom of Lansdown Road) stood St. Werberg's Chapel, dedicated in 1170. The site was evidently one of some antiquity for the dedication document mentions that here already were altars dedicated to St. John the Evangelist and St. Catherine, Virgin and Martyr and to these 'the faithful throng with great veneration'. Clearly the spot was one of some sanctity going back to Saxon times, but its origins must remain obscure. One possibility, however, is that it might have grown up on the site of the burial of a Christian martyr of the Roman period: it is

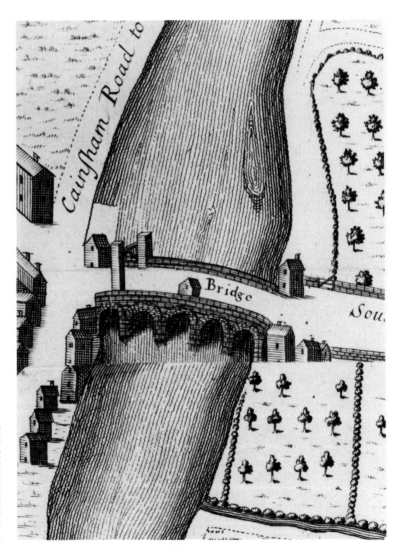

60. The city bridge at the end of Southgate Street was probably built in the early medieval period – perhaps by John of Tours, and remained largely untouched throughout the Middle Ages. Seen here in Gilmore's map of 1694.

in the area of one of the Roman cemeteries of the town, but otherwise the suggestion is pure speculation.

To the south of the river, along the Holloway leading up Beechen cliff from the bridge lay the Hospital of St. Mary Magdalen, founded originally as a hospital for poor lepers, conveniently well away from the urban community. In the later Middle Ages the site became a private chapel for the priors of Bath. Its very existence is a reminder both of Bath's attraction as a place of healing and also of the responsibility which the church of the day took for the care of the sick and poor.

In 1379 a poll tax was held in Bath on the accession of Richard II, by which every adult member of the resident community had to pay a sum of money to the state each according to his wealth and status, from 10 marks for a duke down to 4 pence for an ordinary 'general' man. Married couples paid at a single rate. To facilitate collecting the tax every person was listed by name, in the order of the street in which they lived, and the profession of each was recorded. The document, which still survives, gives a vivid insight into the life and fortunes of the late medieval town.

61.   In this water-colour of Bernard Lens (1718) the gate at the south end of the bridge can be seen together with the little oratory of St. Lawrence which stood in the middle of the bridge. Compare it with Gilmore's rendering of 1694. (ill. 60).

62. Bath's first charter was issued by Richard I in 1189. The crucial part reads, 'We have ordained that the citizens of Bath who are of its merchant guild, shall have in all things the same acquittance and freedom for all their merchant goods, wherever they shall go by land or sea, from tolls, payments for bridges, and in markets, and all other customs burdens and things, as fully and freely as have our Citizens of Winchester and their merchant guild, and we forbid anyone to disturb or molest them or their property in this wise, under forfeit of £10'.

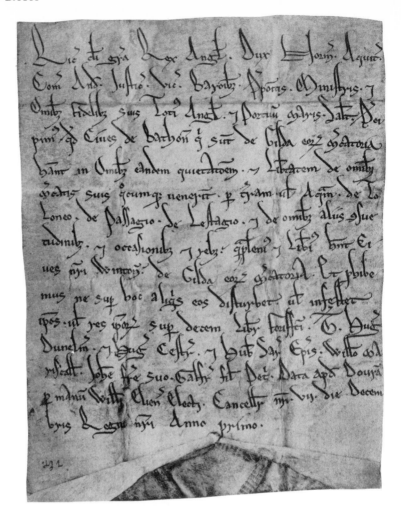

In all some 328 individuals are listed but what is surprising is that of these, 112 resided in the north suburb and 18 in the southern, the remaining 198 living within the walled area. Thus the suburbs, and in particular the north suburb, were by now extremely populous. Within the walls the distribution of houses was by no means uniform. The most heavily built-up street was Stall Street (77), the street created as the result of Bishop John's reorganizatiion and getting its name from the temporary stalls built along it just outside the abbey precinct wall. By 1379 these had long since been converted to permanent residences. Next came Northgate Strete (the market street) with 42 while the road from West gate to the southern end of Northgate Street, i.e. Westgate Strete and Sowter Strete, produced 18 and 39 individuals respectively. Of the rest of the streets in the town only the two in the south-west corner, By ye bath Strete and Bynburi Strete, were listed with 13 and 9 individuals. Thus the bulk of the population lived along the two main axes of the city with few elsewhere and no-one occupying the north-eastern corner of the walled area. This is precisely the picture captured 230 years later by Speed's map of 1610.

In terms of total population the poll tax returns suggest a figure of 1100 individuals for Bath at this time but we are looking at a town, and indeed a country, which was just beginning to re-establish its population levels after the devastation of the Black Death forty years or so before. At the beginning of the century the population would have been nearer the 2000 mark and the derelict areas of the town, away from the main streets, would then have been bristling with activity.

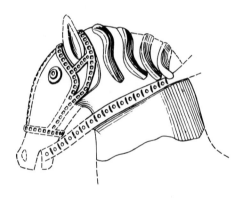

63. Tiled roofs gradually became the norm in medieval Bath. The crests were usually decorated with cockscomb ridge tiles sometimes enlivened with finials. The illustrated fragment is part of a roof finial in the form of a mounted knight. Scale 1:3. (Source: Cunliffe 1979, fig. 69).

The economy of the city throughout the Middle Ages was closely bound up with the fortunes of the two biggest land owners, the bishop and the prior, whose extensive estates, scattered about the countryside, provided the townspeople with the basis of their livelihood. Thus the connection between abbey and town would always have been close. Of considerable importance to the economic well-being of the community was its right to hold fairs. Henry I granted Bishop John the right to hold one on the festival of St. Peter, and later two more annual fairs were approved by Edward I. The fair was the time when local products in surplus could be exchanged for materials and manufactured goods brought in from outside the immediate region. Since medieval Bath, like so many Cotswold towns, owed its prosperity to the wool trade, it is hardly surprising to find the monastery dealing in the commodity. Records are far from adequate but we hear of Prior Thomas buying 300 sacks of

wool in 1334 and then a further 600 sacks three years later from a Marlborough merchant, and since Bath is at no time recorded as an exporter of raw wool to the Flemish and Florentine weavers (as were many other monasteries), the implication is that one of the prime activities of the establishment was spinning and weaving and the subsequent sale of the manufactured cloth. It is significant that the mill, owned by the monks, and sited on the Avon close to the city wall, was a fulling mill essential to the final preparation of the woven fabric. Nor should Chaucer's *Wife of Bath* be forgotten. Her predilection for energetic husbands apart,

> 'Of clooth-making she hadde swiche an haunt,
> She passed hem of Ypres and of Gaunt'.

Interesting light is thrown on the activities of the townspeople in the late fourteenth century by the poll tax returns. Of the 328 individuals listed only 106 were trades or craftsmen, most of the rest being labourers or servants. Of these there were present in the town three weavers, six fullers, eleven spinners and eight tailors and a number of the artificers, several of whom were quite wealthy men with servants. Many of them were probably also involved in the wool trade. The only other activity of any significance was connected with leather working. One tanner, two skinners and eight shoe makers are recorded. There is no evidence that the town was geared up for a tourist market. Only two hostlers appear and no-one is specifically mentioned as being involved with the baths.

As to the distribution of wealth, there were 19 people paying a tax of 2 shillings or more: two lived in the southern suburb and 5 in the northern suburb. The rest lived within the walled area along the four main streets. Of the four richest men in town, paying 5 shillings or more, two lived in Northgate Street, one in Broad Street while the address of the other, the mayor, is not given. Although the figures cannot be forced too far, the walled area certainly contained a higher proportion of the better off than the suburbs – a pattern which continued into the seventeenth century (p. 11) – but worked out on a per capita value for each street, Southgate Street was the most wealthy, Bynburi and By ye Bath Streets the poorest, and the rest were at much the same median level.

For Bath the medieval period was a time of considerable change. It had begun in the late eleventh century with the large-scale replanning of the town and its suburbs, and the massive rebuilding programme in the newly created monastic precinct, and throughout the twelfth and early thirteenth centuries prosperity was at its height. But with the lack of interest in Bath shown by the later bishops, the monastic community lost its drive. The Black Death in the early part of the fourteenth century devastated the religious and secular communities alike, but the increasing corporate powers of the townspeople and the feeling of civic identity that emerged ensured that the economy continued to develop, irrespective of the decline of the priory, and for much of the fourteenth and fifteenth centuries Bath passed its days as a comfortable and moderately prosperous little wool town, fitting comfortably into the urban framework that John of Tours had laid out for it centuries before. Only in the priory itself was there change to be seen, for by the end of the fourteenth century with its complement of monks down to only 21, it had a very run down appearance. In 1499 Bishop Oliver King visited the establishment and was far from pleased with what he saw: discipline was, to say the least, lax. There was feasting in the refectory, the monks were idle and women were often to be seen at unseemly times about the precinct of the monastery. In addition the church was now so neglected as to be a near ruin. In this *fin de siecle* atmosphere, a major era in Bath's history was rapidly nearing an end.

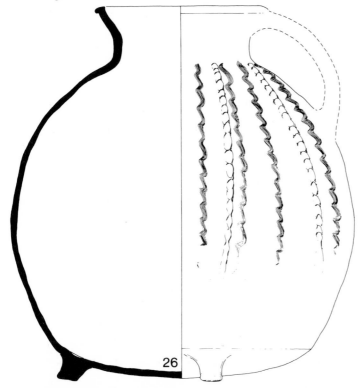

64. Bath's medieval pottery was of high quality. This green glazed pitcher comes from an excavation on the site of St. John's Hospital. Scale 1:4 (Source: Cunliffe 1979, fig. 64).

5. DISSOLUTION AND AFTER:
THE SIXTEENTH AND SEVENTEENTH CENTURIES

BISHOP KING'S visit to Bath in 1499 in many ways symbolizes the end of the Middle Ages. The monastic establishment, he found, was morally lax, verging on the decadent, while the great medieval cathedral priory, began by John of Tours four hundred years earlier, was fast decaying through age and neglect. So began the sixteenth century. The two centuries to follow, 1500–1700, was a time of dramatic social upheaval. The dissolution of the monasteries was followed a century later by Civil War, and Bath, in company with many other small towns, came through it all physically changed but without significant growth: indeed the medieval town plan is virtually indistinguishable from the plan at the very beginning of the eighteenth century. Yet the city was a very different place, for what had before been totally dominated by the church was now wholly in the hands of the city's corporate body: the bishop and the prior had been replaced by the mayor and the corporation. Institutions and buildings alike reflected this upheaval and by 1700 Bath was on the threshold of a spectacular period of urban growth.

At the time of Bishop King's visit in the last year of the fifteenth century few can have foreseen the dramatic changes which the next forty years were to hold, least of all King himself, for he enthusiastically set about the complete restoration of the monastic establishment. A strict order was re-established and £300 of the priory's annual revenue of £480 was set aside for repairing and rebuilding. This project was entrusted to the newly appointed prior, William Birde.

Prior Birde decided to rebuild completely the priory church – a vast task which entailed the virtual demolition of the twelfth-century church and its replacement with a smaller building covering only the nave of its predecessor. Birde died in 1525 when work was still in progress, but rebuilding continued unhindered under his successor William Holleway (alias Gybbs).

The new building was one of quality. The masons employed were Robert and William Vertue both of whom also worked for the king. They had completed Henry VII's chapel at Westminster Abbey by 1512 and William, after his brother's death, went on to build St. George's Chapel, Windsor. They were masters of fan vaulting and it was clear that they intended that Bath priory should be so adorned. The choir vault was finished in their time but the nave vault was not completed until 1869! – a reminder that the great building was still unfinished by

M.r Fords Lodgings in Stauls Street

the time of the Dissolution in 1535 and what we see today is the result of later generations doing their best to anticipate the original intentions of the early sixteenth century architects.

In the summer of 1535 Dr. Richard Layton arrived in Bath to gather material for his Black Book of Monasteries which was designed to provide Thomas Cromwell with the evidence he needed to justify their dissolution. Layton's report on Bath to the Vicar-General is not without interest, even though we should always bear in mind that his comments were necessarily biased against the monks.

> 'Hit may please yor godness to understand that we have visited Bathe wheras we found the prior a right virtuose man and I suppose no better of his cote, a man simple and not of the gretesteste wit, his monkes worse than I have any fownde yet both in bugerie and adulterie sum one of them having x women sum viii and the reste so fewer. The house well repared but foure hundreth powndes in dett'.

He goes on to say that the prior was sending Cromwell some Irish hawkes – evidently intended as a gentle bribe. Layton also wished to ingratiate himself with Cromwell and had no qualms about giving him a rare book purloined from the monastic library described somewhat enigmatically as 'a bowke of Or Lades miracles well able to mache the canterberie tailles'.

It was the beginning of the end for the monks, and although the convent was allowed to continue for a further four years the monks were under virtual house-arrest, forbidden to leave the precinct. A month after Layton's visit Prior Holleway wrote to Cromwell to seek permission to defend a court action, adding to his request, 'I have send yor maistershipp hereyn an old Boke Opera Anselmi whiche one William Tildysleye after scrutinye made here in my libarye willed me to send unto youe . . .' another thinly disguised bribe. Worse was to follow. In 1537 Cromwell was thanked for protecting the prior against some undefined hostile act, and the opportunity was taken to offer him a pension of £5 yearly, but Cromwell's mind was made up and all must have realized that the monastery had little time left.

It was in this atmosphere of impending closure that Prior Holleway began to disperse the holdings and property of the establishment, making over leases of estates, small holdings, houses and cottages and much else to the influential families of the town and region – no doubt in keen anticipation of their continued favour and support. Holleway realized that when, eventually, the monastic property was confiscated by the Crown

The three Tunns Sodomes by the Kings Bath

65. The West elevation of the Abbey church drawn by Daniel King *c.* 1640.

the king would feel it necessary to leave the gifts as they were rather than risk alienating the local gentry. Thus in the one gesture the monks had bought friends and frustrated the State.

The end came on 27 January 1539 when Dr. Tregonwell and Dr. Petre arrived in Bath to receive the surrender of the priory. There was no contest or resistance and the final deed was signed by the prior, the sub-prior and eighteen monks bringing to an end nearly 900 years of monastic tradition. The inmates were fairly treated. Prior Holleway was given a substantial pension of £80 a year together with a house in Stall Street worth 20 shillings a year, the rest received pensions of between £4 13s 4d and £9 according to status and some took up parish duties. A local tradition has it that Holleway – who was something of an alchemist – salvaged the monastery's supply of stores, medicines and elixirs and secreted them in a wall from which hiding place they were stolen. The shock was such that the old man went blind and mad. He ended his years wandering around the country led by a boy.

The early sixteenth century was a time of much academic excitement. The ancient monastic libraries, for long inaccessible, were now being opened up to an enquiring world, travel was becoming easier and there was a quite new interest in the topography of the countryside. A man in the forefront of this

66.   The South elevation of the Abbey church drawn by Daniel King *c.* 1640. The abbey church was a sixteenth century creation. It was not properly finished until the late ninteenth century. Note that the nave was at this time without flying buttresses.

awakening was John Leland, a schoolmaster-scholar who in 1533 received a warrant from the king, Henry VIII, to search the monastic and collegiate libraries so that the works of ancient writers 'mighte be brought owte of deadly darkness to Lyvely Lighte'. While travelling about the country searching libraries he developed a passion for topographical studies writing to the king, 'I was totally inflamed with a love to see thoroughly all those parts of this your opulent and ample realm . . . . I have travelled your dominions both by the sea coasts and the middle parts, sparing neither labour nor costs by the space of these 6 years past . . . . I have seen them, and noted in doing so a whole world of things very memorable'. The results of his travels were eventually published, much later, as *The Itinerary of John Leland*.

Leland visited Bath twice, before and after the surrender of the priory, and provides a vivid description of the little town. Coming from the south, down Holloway, he crossed the medieval bridge with its 'great gate with a stone arch', and then travel led up Southgate Street, marking 'fair Medowes on Eche Hand', to enter the town via the South gate. 'The Cite of Bath is sette booth yn a fruteful and pleasant Botom, the which is environid on every side with greate Hilles out of which cum many Springes of pure Water that be coveyid by dyverse ways to serve the Cite. Insomuch that Leade beyng made ther at hand many Houses yn the Toune have Pipes of Leade to convey Water from Place to Place'. Piped water was evidently something of a novelty at the time.

Leland goes on to describe in loving, and fascinating, detail the city gates and the walls, patched with a variety of Roman carvings and inscriptions, the baths and the monastic buildings. His description of the thriving church was written a year or so after the Dissolution. 'Oliver King bisshop of Bath began of late dayes a right goodly new chirch at the west part of the olde church of S. Peter and finished a great peace of it. The residue of it was sins made by the priors of Bath: and especially by Gibbes the last prior ther that spent a great summe of mony on that Fabrike. Oliver King let almost al the old chirch of S. Peter's in Bath to go ruins. The walles yet stande'. He goes on to tell us that in the weed-grown ruins of the old medieval building still standing to the east of the new church, he found the tomb of Bishop John and another great marble tomb – 'There were other divers bisshops buried there'. The newly finished building standing amid the ruins of its larger predecessor must have been an odd sight – a moment of change, fossilized by the Dissolution.

The priory lands, now in the hands of the Crown, were sold

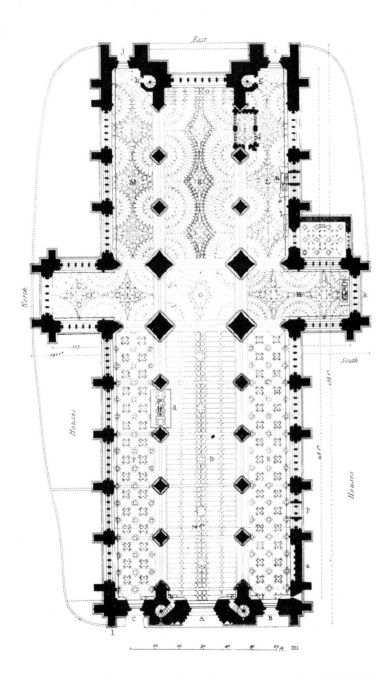

67. The architectual finesse of the abbey church can best be appreciated from this detailed plan published by J. Britton in 1816. At this time the nave was without fan vaulting. The present vault, copying that of the choir, was added by Gilbert Scott in the 1869.

off by Cromwell's commission. The church was offered to the city for 500 marks but the citizens were suspicious of such a cheap deal and turned it down. As a result the building was gutted: lead, glass, iron and bells were removed and sold as scrap leaving the shell of the building to go to ruin. Meanwhile the materials of the dormitory were bought by Robert Cocks, the frater by Sir Walter Denys and the cloisters by Henry Bewchyn. After the demolition contractors had finished there was little left of the claustral buildings except for the old west range, the prior's lodging, which now became a private residence called Abbey House (ill. 75).

The carcass of the church, together with the priory lands, were sold to a wealthy local landowner, Humphry Colles. A little later the church passed to Matthew Colthurst whose son, Edmund, presented it to the citizens of Bath, in 1560, to become their parish church. The rest of the precinct was sold off in 1569, and eventually came into the hands of the Duke of Kingston and Earl Manvers, whose names will appear again in the next chapter in the story of the eighteenth-century developers.

The passing of the priory properties into the hands of individual landowners and under the control of the city authorities was quickly followed by the bishop's desire to be rid of his properties in Bath and accordingly in 1548 he gave all his possessions in the city to Edward VI in exchange for equivalent lands elsewhere. To begin with the corporation, who collected the fees, passed them to the king, but gradually concessions were made and in 1590 Elizabeth granted the city a new charter of incorporation. As a result all the powers of the bishop and prior were now vested in the civic authority.

The new men were tough entrepreneurs intent on establishing the well-being of their city – and in doing so ensuring their own increasing fortunes. The story of the sixteenth century is one of continuous take-over as the city strove to bring property and patronage alike under its single control. Elizabeth's charter not only bestowed full powers of government on the mayor, aldermen and citizens but it also greatly extended the bounds of the city, adding to the old walled town substantial areas in the neighbourhood, including the whole of the Barton Farm to the north-west and a large part of the parish of Walcot. This provided space to expand when, with the Civil War over, Bath began to prosper and to grow. The shell of the gutted abbey church did not long remain uncared for for long. In 1572 the citizens of Bath petitioned for the abbey church to become their parish church, absorbing the three city centre parishes of St.

The Hart Lodgings in Stall Street

Mary de Stalle, St. Mary *intra muros* and St. Michael's. It was a logical move and the licence was granted. Thereupon the abbey was reconsecrated and dedicated to SS Peter and Paul. As a result the two churches of St. Mary gradually became redundant and were secularized, though St. Mary de Stalle, once the principal church of the city, was still being used for worship in 1593, the final transfer to the abbey taking place in 1606.

With its new-found status as parish church of the city centre, the abbey was gradually renovated (ill. 65). In 1572 a citizen put up sufficient money for the repair of the east end and the north aisle, and not long afterwards Queen Elizabeth authorized a nation-wide collection, over a period of seven years. The money raised paid for further reroofing and for the reglazing of some of the windows. But the task of making the building fully serviceable was still far from complete. In 1603 Mr. Bellot added sufficiently to earlier endowments he had made so that the transept could be completed but as a contemporary critic wrote, 'The Church lies still like the poore traveller . . . spoild and wounded by thieves. The Priest goes by, the Levites go by but do nothing: only a good Samaritan, honest Mr. Billet (*sic*) . . . hath powr'd some oyle in the wounds and maintained it in life'. Its final restoration was entirely due to Bishop James Montague, Bishop of Bath and Wells from 1608–1616, who throughout his episcopate forced on the work, at a cost of £1000. The citizens of Bath could face the seventeenth century with a fine parish church, far too large for parochial needs, but redolent of the spirit of the city and its new-found corporate identity.

The priory had taken upon itself responsibility for the poor and the sick. St. John's Hospital, St. Katherine's Hospital and the Hospital of St. Mary Magdalen – all medieval foundations – had provided a much needed community service. The way in which they developed after the Dissolution provides an interesting example of the transformation now taking place. St. John's Hospital managed to escape the suppression of 1539 and in 1573 was transferred to the control of the corporation. Queen Elizabeth authorized the collection of money for the charity and sufficient funds were raised to rebuild the old structure as a single-storeyed colonnaded building. Later another storey was added to provide letting accommodation for visitors in order to augment the income of the establishment (ill. 68). Here indeed was entrepreneurial flair, best explained when it is realized that St. John's was now vested in the mayor and citizens and that for a while at least the mayor was also the hospital's master. This was only a beginning and under the patronage of the Duke of

68. St. John's Hospital, a medieval foundation, in Gilmore's view.

Chandos the early eighteenth century was to see further development and exploitation all of which was, and still is, of direct benefit to the original charity.

Close to St. John's was the Hospital of St. Katherine's fronting on to Binbury Lane. It seems to have been founded in the early fifteenth century and though a purely secular establishment it was surrendered at the time of the Dissolution, but remained a municipal charity vested in the mayor and citizens. In 1552 Edward VI returned unsold monastic property to the city, requiring the income to be shared between the hospital and a new school, which was established just outside the Northgate. The hospital remained on its original site until 1825 when it was moved to allow for the construction of the Royal United Hospital.

The two medieval hospitals in the city benefited considerably when control of their affairs passed to the city, but St. Mary Magdalen, on the southern approach road, was the scene of interminable wrangles. The foundation had originally cared for the leprous poor but seems to have suffered from the disputes of the sixteenth century. It was probably against this background that, in 1576, John de Feckenham, the last abbot of Westminster, built the Lepers' Bath immediately adjacent to the Hot Bath (ill. 74). It was described by John Wood, the man responsible for its demolition in 1776, as 'being the place of resource for the most miserable objects that seek relief from the healing fountains . . . it is proportionately mean, obscure and small' – a description which fits well with Guidott's illustration

69. The hospitals for the sick and poor in Bath were situated in the south-western corner of the city close to the Cross and Hot Baths. St. Katherine's and Bellots Hospitals were of Renaissance date. Bellots Hospital is seen here in 1845.

of 1691. Nonetheless for those suffering from the wide variety of skin diseases prevalent at the time it would have been a haven of hope.

The last of the charitable establishments to occupy the south-west quarter of the old town was Bellots Hospital (ills. 69–70) established in Binbury Lane in 1608 by the philanthropic Thomas Bellott who had already contributed much to the repair of the abbey church. The almshouses were established for 'such poor diseased persons being not infected with any contageous disease as shall resorte and come to the said City of Bathe' up to the number of 12. In 1652 another endowment allowed a physician to be appointed to care for the health of the inmates. The original building consisted of a courtyard surrounded by single-storeyed ranges divided into fourteen rooms. The hospital was rebuilt between 1859 and 1864 and still continues to serve the intentions of its founder.

A place with the reputation of Bath for cure and care soon became a haven for the destitute. As one contemporary writer put it so succinctly, 'Many beggars in that place, some natives there, others repairing thither from all parts of the land, the poor for alms, the pained for ease'. With its four almshouses and baths for the diseased Bath was unusually well provided. Those simply suffering from the 'cramp of laziness' were rounded up by the authority of the Poor Law Act of 1601 and confined to the Bridewell, or house of correction, situated at the north end of Bridewell Lane close to the city wall, there to be maintained and made to work. The same act also allowed part of the poor rate to be used to provide food and clothing for the genuinely needy and to pay for their shrouds and graves when they ceased to be a burden on the parish officers.

But the sick and needy were not the only visitors to Bath. The sixteenth century saw a growing tide of middle and upper class travellers arriving in the city to enjoy the curative waters the benefits of which were now beginning to be widely marketed by an increasingly aware corporation and a clutch of physicians, of varying degrees of respectability, prepared to offer their services and advice to those seeking the cure. People had visited the baths in the medieval period but now they came in seasonal swarms. The reasons were complex, but foremost must have been the increasing ease of movement in England, and the corresponding insecurity of travel on the Continent, racked by the Religious Wars. Another factor was undoubtedly the flood of medieval writings which, in the latter part of the sixteenth century, were begining to extol the virtues of bathing. The first was by Dr. William Turner (in the latter part of his eventful life

Part of Billot. Hospitall

70. Bellots Hospital by Gilmore in 1694.

Dean of Wells). In a book dealing with the baths of England, Germany and Italy, published in 1557, he says quite unashamedly, 'I have also writen so well as I can of the bath of Baeth in England to allure thyther as manye as have nede of suche helpe as almighty God hath graunted it to gyve'. This was soon followed by John Jones' volume, published 1572, entitled 'The Bathes of Bathes Ayde wonderfull and most excellent agaynst very many Sicknesses, approved by authoritie, confirmed by reason, and dayly tried by experience'. At about the same time (at least before 1585) Abbot Fakenham, in his 'Book of sovereigne medicines', gives an account of 'Prescriptions and rules to be observed att the Bathe'. And so it goes on throughout the seventeenth and eighteenth centuries – one volume after another. Hypochondriacs of the day can have been left in no doubt that it was to Bath that they must travel.

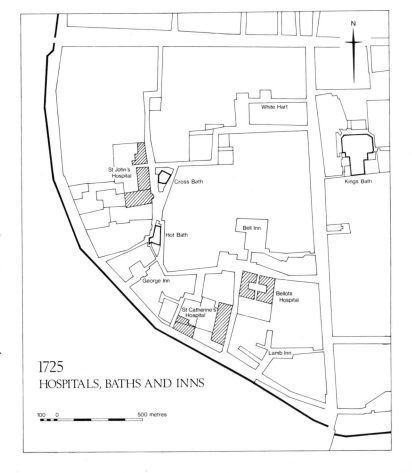

71. The south-west corner of the city was a clutter of buildings and small alleyways. The two baths – the Cross Bath and Hot Bath – were less fashionable than the King's Bath and attracted the poor and infirm. Three hospitals to care for the poor grew up nearby: St. John's, St. Katherine's and Bellots. The quarter was also well provided with hotels. The map is redrawn from a survey of 1725 and shows the city before the great development of the eighteenth century. (Source: author).

1725
HOSPITALS, BATHS AND INNS

100 0   500 metres

The three baths which they saw had probably changed very little since the early medieval period. The King's Bath, so brilliantly captured in Thomas Johnson's pen and wash drawing of 1675 (ill. 72), was still essentially in its medieval form, with the main pool surrounded by arched recesses as it had been since the early twelfth century. There were of course embellishments: the elegant balustrade was probably that donated by Sir Francis Stonor who, 'trubled with the gout and aches in the limbs receieved benefit by ye bath', and put up the money for the work in about 1624. The ornamental structure, over the central spring, which came to be known as the Kitchen, was erected in 1578. Next to the King's Bath was a second smaller bath, built in about 1576 to extend the facilities by providing a cooler bath for those who required it: it was filled directly with the overflow from the King's Bath. Known first as the New Bath, it acquired the name of Queen's Bath following the visits of Queen Anne of Denmark, wife of James I, in 1613 and 1615.

72.   Thomas Johnson's illustration of the King's Bath in 1675 gives a brilliantly detailed and lively picture of the centre of the city before the great eighteenth century rebuilding. Virtually all the houses around the baths are of sixteenth and seventeenth century date and most were lodging houses. The baths were open and evidently provided a focus of entertainment for idlers. The arched recesses in the King's Bath were part of the original medieval arrangement to provide seats and shelter for the bathers.

The bathers of this period disported themselves in full gaze of the idle public. Dressing and undressing was achieved in the comparative privacy of either the entrance passages (slips), which led down from street level to the water at each of the four corners, or in the cramped dressing rooms attached to them. John Wood, writing in the mid-eighteenth century, gives a somewhat jaundiced, but one suspects not inaccurate, impression of the general scruffiness of it all when he says, 'The Baths were like so many Bear Gardens, and Modesty was entirely shut out of them; People of both Sexes bathing by Day and Night naked; and Dogs, Cats, and even human creatures were hurl'd over the rails into the water, while People were bathing in it'.

The two other baths in the south-west corner of the town were also popular. The Cross Bath was the larger of the two frequented, as Leland tells us, by 'People diseasid with Lepre, Pokkes, Scabbes and great Aches'. Thomas Johnson, writing in the mid-seventeenth century, gives a brief description, 'almost triangular, twenty-five feet long and of equal breddth at the widest part. It has arched seats on all sides, three dressing-rooms and as many flights of steps. It is surrounded by a wall. The springs here are smaller than in the Kings and Hot and it is therefore not so hot'. Guidott's elegant plan from his *De Thermis* (1691) provides an exceptionally clear impression of the scale and layout (ill. 91).

The Hot Bath, which lay to the south, was, according to Leland quite small – 'lesse in Cumpace withyn the Waulle then

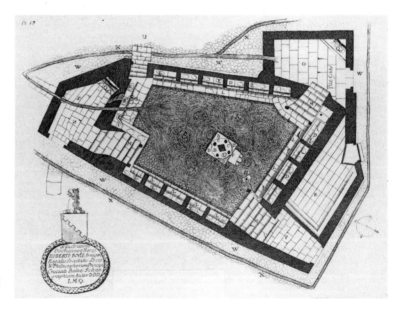

73. The Cross Bath as depicted by Guidott in 1691.

the other, having but 7 Arches yn the Waulle'. But towards the end of the sixteenth century it was enlarged, resulting in a lowering of the overall temperature. Guidott's plan shows the enlarged building with its rectangular pool surrounded by a wall containing recesses down the long sides. Three entrances came directly from the street, but at both ends were dressing rooms with their own flights of steps leading down to the water. These may be the private baths referred to in contemporary legal documents. The other feature of Guidott's plan is the small bath attached to the west wall. This is the Lepers' Bath built by Abbot Feckenham in or soon after 1576. The Hot Bath had originally been open to all, diseased and poor alike, but in the improvements undertaken by the corporation in the late sixteenth century the bath had been both enlarged and gentrified. Feckenham's little bath and the nearby Leper Hospital was an act of benevolence designed to ensure that those in need continued to have some access to the curative waters.

The third quarter of the sixteenth century was a vital period in the development of the spa. In Letters Patent of 1552 the mayor and citizens of Bath were granted all the property within the city previously owned by the priory. Then followed a series of legal wrangles as the city doggedly established its rights. By 1568, when the Chamberlain's Accounts begin, the corporation was

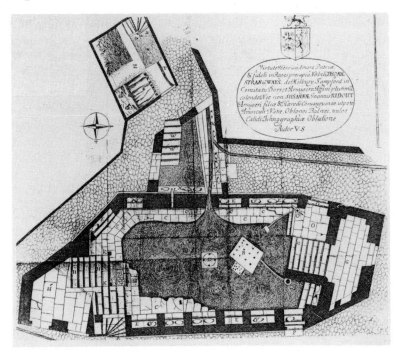

74. The Hot Bath by Guidott. The small room opening off the Hot Bath was a facility specially constructed for lepers.

fully in control of all the city's major assets and the development of the baths was given new impetus. The sixteenth century, then, was a turning point – a time when Bath shook off its dependence on wool production and began consciously to establish itself as a tourist centre: it was the beginning of the present era.

Increases in visitor numbers meant that new facilities had to be created to entertain and to house them. That the city entrepreneurs responded to the need is made clear by the comments of several visitors, 'The City of Bath being both poor enough and proud enough, hath since her Highness being there (1574) wonderfully beautified itself in fine houses for victualling and lodging' and again, 'The buildings of the city are sufficiently numerous, large and commodious for the reception of the stream of sick persons from all parts who, seeking the cure of their diseases flock hither annually in Spring and Autumn. . .'.

Royal or noble visitors chose to stay in either Westgate House, situated, as its name implied, on the city wall, next to the West gate, or in Abbey House, a modernized version of the monastic priors' lodging. For the rest they could choose between lodging houses, often run by the city's physicians, or one of the dozen or so hotels which had sprung up. There were three in Stall Street, close to the King's Bath: The White Heart, The Cross Bow and The Three Tuns, and three more just around the corner in Cheap Street: The Raven, The Bear and The Lower (or White) Swan. The Bell and The George were conveniently near the Hot Bath. The rest were scattered about with three in the northern suburb. The little vignettes on the borders of Gilmore's map of 1694 (ill. 76) show them to be

75. Gilmore's map provides vignettes of the various lodging houses where visitors to the baths could stay. Many were run by local doctors. The Abbey House was where royalty and the aristocracy frequently chose to stay. It had originally been the Abbot's Lodging of the medieval monastery and occupied the entire west range of the claustral buildings: it is all that survived the Reformation.

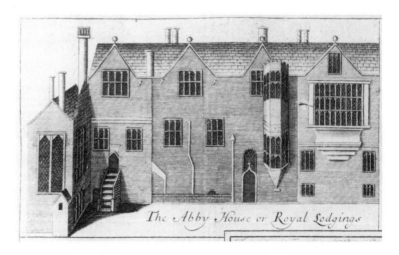

The Abby House or Royal Lodgings

large well-appointed structures new-built in the style of the
times. In the confines of the little town with its narrow medieval
streets, these new three-storeyed houses must have created an
almost claustrophobic feeling and yet they seem to have pleased
the visitors, 'Bath is a little well-compacted Cittie and beautified
with very faire and goodly buildings for receipt of strangers'.

Visitors also needed recreation and in this they were well
provided. Bowling was popular. By the end of the seventeenth
century a large plot of land to the south-east of the abbey church
had become a bowling green (ill. 81). An earlier account refers
to there being two greens in the area, one of them 'curiously and
neatly kept where onely Lords, Knights, Gallants and Gen-
tlemen, of the best ranke, and qualitie doe dayly meet . . . to
recreate themselves, both for pleasure, and health'. Gilmore's
map (1694) shows a 'New bowling Green' evidently carved out
of the rear ends of a number of tenement plots to the west of
Broad Street some short distance outside the north wall. There
was also a Fives Court just outside the West gate and it is
possible that the tennis court (for real-tennis) shown on Speed's
map of 1610 just east of the King's Bath, was still in existence.
In addition to these more strenuous pursuits there was ample
space to walk at leisure in the old abbey gardens between the
east wall and the river, or to attend theatrical performances held
in the Guildhall or in the courtyards of the larger inns. For a
town of its size seventeenth-century Bath was exceptionally well
provisioned for the entertainment of its visitors. As Sir Edmund
Verney rather plaintively put it, 'We pass our time awaye as
merrily as paine will give us leave'.

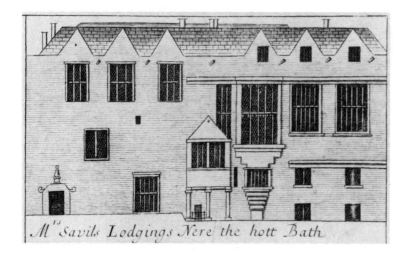

76. Mrs Savils
Lodgings near to the
Hot Bath from
Gilmore's map 1694.

Aside from the visitors Bath continued to develop its commercial aspects as a small but quite prosperous market town. Central to this activity was the market place at the south end of High Street where, in the medieval period, the temporary stalls of the local traders were put up on market days. In its new-found affluence the town began to formalize these arrangements in a market hall, built *c.* 1551, in the centre of the place. At this time the Guildhall was a separate building standing nearby on the east side of High Street but in 1625 the old market hall was swept away and an elegant new Guildhall and market hall were erected in its place (ill. 77). According to tradition it was built after a design by Inigo Jones but there is no direct proof that this was so. The rapid change during this brief period is a reflection of the pace and energy with which Bath's economy was developing.

The acquisition of the priory and the bishop's property by the city authorities meant that the corporation was now able to impose what terms it wished on those holding leases on corporate property. Some of the terms required specific services of the lessee, such as the repair of the road in front of their houses or the regular cleaning of the general environment, but there were also more general terms imposed to improve the city as a whole. For example in the early seventeenth century it was a general requirement 'that every person that hath a thatched house shall not mend his house with thatch but shall repair it with tyle or slate'. The effect of this simple clause on the appearance of the city would have been dramatic. Johnson's drawing gives a vivid idea of the quality of the city centre at the end of the seventeenth century with its two-storey medieval houses, now tiled, fast being dwarfed by new four-storey residences packed tightly into the old medieval burgage plots with space to expand only upwards. But the effects of progress were not wholly beneficial – 'a multitude of chimneys arose – and there did arise so many dusty clouds in the air as to hide the light of the sun'. Bath began to learn that people pollute.

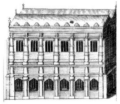

77. The market was held at the south end of High Street which widened for the purpose. In 1625 a fine Guild Hall was built to replace an earlier sixteenth century structure on the same site. John Wood said that the new Guild Hall was 'erected after a draught by Inigo Jones' but there is no proof that this was so. The illustration is from Gilmore's map.

Rubbish was still being dumped in the streets or thrown over the wall as late as the early seventeenth century. In 1613, however, a scavenger was appointed and citizens were required to take their rubbish to the scavenger's cart as he passed through the streets. But not all obeyed and in 1633 it was 'ordered that everyone that doth strike or sweep the streete before their dores and putt it into ye channel' (i.e. the open culverts that ran through the streets at this time) 'shall pay xijd for each offence'. Twenty years later John Evelyn could still describe the streets as 'narrow, uneven and unpleasant'. But the most lively description of the streets of the city at the turn of the century is given by John Wood, the man soon to be responsible for the city's transformation. 'The streets and public ways of the city were become like so many dunghills, slaughter house, pig styes: for soil of all sorts, and even carrion, were cast and laid in the streets, and the pigs turned out by day to feed and rout among it; butchers killed and dressed their cattle at their own doors; people washed every kind of thing they had to make clean at the common conduits in the open streets; and nothing was more common than small racks and mangers at almost every door for the baiting of horses'.

Throughout the sixteenth and seventeenth centuries the population seems to have remained relatively steady and much as it was in the late fourteenth century. The Lay Subsidy Return of 1524 and 5, which listed all people owning land or goods to the value of 40s a year and all with wages of 20s a year or more, gives between 200 and 250 names suggesting a total population

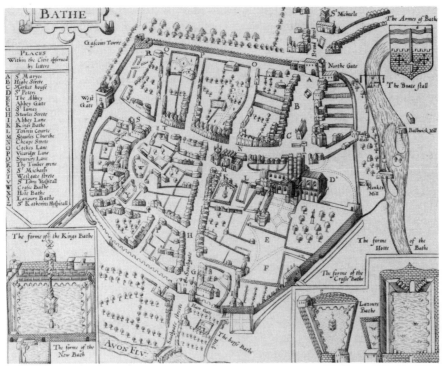

78.   Speed's map of Bath, published in 1610 as an inset to his county map, gives a vivid impression of the small late medieval town still largely contained within its walls. Most of the street frontages were heavily built up but there was ample space in the town provided by the back gardens. The abbey precinct had not yet been developed.

of in the order of 1200. A survey of corporate property in 1641 (and the corporation owned virtually all the city property) lists 300 houses, which allowing 3–5 people per house, gives a total of between 900 and 1500 inhabitants. But that there was a steady growth in population is suggested by the statistics derived from the parish registers for the period 1569–1625. Christenings averaged 48 per year, deaths were at the rate of 44 per year. In other words, the increase of christenings over burials, over a 50 year period, was in the order of 240. By the end of the century, allowing for servants, beggars and visitors the population must have been about 2000.

The seventeenth century saw a growing disparity in the distribution of wealth in the city and this is reflected in the Hearth Tax Assessment of 1664–5. The tax was based on the number of hearths owned by each household and is therefore a fair reflection of the relative wealth of the individual establishments. Binbury Lane seems now to have become the most

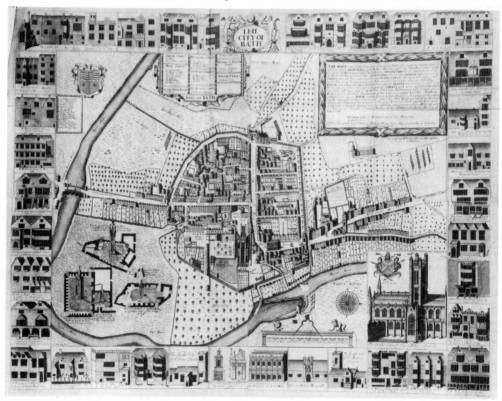

79.   Gilmore's map of 1694 is more detailed than Speed's but shows how little urban expansion there was in the seventeenth century. It was however a time of much rebuilding within the city walls. Joseph Gilmore was a teacher of mathematics in the city of Bristol.

prosperous area (7.3 hearths per house). The rest of the walled area seems to have been of lower status: Westgate Street (4.8), Stall Street (4.5), Cheap Street (4.3) and Northgate Street (3.5). The poorer district were now those outside the walls with the north suburb averaging 2.8 and the south as low as 1.9. To some extent these extramural areas would have suffered more than the projected core from the effects of the Civil War sieges and this would account for their decline but the general trend was probably established well before.

At this time Bath was still very much a walled city and indeed secure walls had stood the citizens in good stead during the Civil War. When Samuel Pepys visited Bath in 1668 he spent a while 'walking round the walls of the city, which are good, and the battlements all whole' but within a mere 50 years they were totally redundant and a barrier to progress.

There is no better way to visualize the little town and to assess the powers which were gathering to transform it, than to compare the two seventeenth century maps – Speed's published in 1610 and Gilmore's of 1694 (ills. 78 and 79). The walls remained largely unchanged but within, the town was beginning to fill up, especially the northern part which in Speed's time had been largely open gardens except along the main street frontages. The density of building around the narrow winding lanes of the south-western sector had also considerably increased, while the old precinct of the abbey and the Bishop's Close, a series of gardens and closes in Speed's time dominated by the church with its ragged unfinished east end, had been formalized as tree-lined walks and bowling greens into which the fingers of building development were beginning to thrust. Outside the walls the poor south suburb remained much the same throughout the seventeenth century, but the northern suburb was now showing definite signs of expansion westwards into the paddocks and closes behind the houses of the Broad Street frontage. The seventeenth century had begun with the town still largely of two-storeyed houses, many of them thatched, set along the streets with large gardens behind – it had ended a burgeoning city of four-storeyed buildings, tiled or slated, fast colonizing the empty spaces of the plots behind the main frontages. Looking at Gilmore's map one cannot help feeling that Bath, at the end of the seventeenth century, was ready to burst out of its walls.

Mr William Chapman's Lodgings by the Kings Bath

6. ELEGANCE AND EXPANSION: THE EIGHTEENTH CENTURY

AT THE BEGINNING of the eighteenth century Bath was still, in physical form, a medieval city, constricted within its walls and packed tight along its alley-like streets. Just 100 years later it had become an elegant sprawl, its terraces and crescents draped with a langorous ease in great strand-lines of urban advance across the valley and up the hills on all sides. At the beginning of the century the population was just over 2000 – in 1801 it was 28,000. This was Bath's industrial revolution – its industry was tourism.

That the city's springs and baths were worthy of public attention was the message which was being broadcast widely throughout the seventeenth century by the local property-owning doctors eager for trade, and trade indeed there was in increasing volume, but to prosper – to take off on a new trajectory – Bath needed to establish itself as a watering place, a 'valley of pleasure' where the wealthy – royalty, the aristocracy and the gentry – would come for relaxation and for fun. The trend had already begun: the itinerant Queen Elizabeth had visited the town twice in 1574 and 1591 and the royal family continued to come throughout the seventeenth century on no less than seven occasions, but it was the last of these, the visit of Princess Anne in 1692, that was to set the seal on Bath's success. Anne evidently approved of the city and returned again in 1702 and 1703, this time as Queen, amid great celebrations,

80. The first Pump Room was built by John Harvey in 1706 in the form of an orangery. The original building was a simple four-bayed structure one of the bays giving access from the abbey yard down to the King's Bath. J. Fayram's view of 1738 captures the simple elegance of the building. Later in 1752 a further bay was added and the roof heightened.

81.   The central area of Bath as depicted by Gilmore in 1694 immediately before the period of expansion began. The two open spaces, the Abbey Garden and the Old Bowling Green occupy the site of the cloisters and east range of the Norman cathedral priory. The crossing and east end of the priory church were on the site of Gravel Walks, later to be known as the Orange Grove.

stage-managed by a city Corporation eager to make it a glittering occasion. Wherever the court went the crowds followed: they liked what they found and almost overnight Bath became fashionable – a watering place of charm set in attractive landscape and within comparatively easy reach of London.

Fashion, however, is a flighty creature and needs to be nurtured. As Oliver Goldsmith said of Bath and other English spas, 'The pleasures they afforded were merely rural; the company splenetic, rustic and vulgar . . . . People of fashion had no agreeable summer retreat from the town (London) . . . . They wanted some place where they might have each other's company, and win each other's money as they had done during the winter in town'. In other words to maintain its allure for the idle rich Bath had to become a gambling town of elegance, more a Monaco than a Las Vegas.

It was at this crucial moment that Richard Nash discovered Bath. As a follower of smart society he came in the wake of Queen Anne: as a highly social creature and born gamester he saw his opportunity and grasped it. This man with 'too much merit not to become remarkable' and 'too much folly to arrive at greatness' (Goldsmith again) was to dominate Bath society for more than half a century. It was he more than anyone else who created and maintained in Bath a social allure irresistible to the pleasure-seeking rich. In turn it was their needs for accommodation and their demands for amusement which provided the motive force to generate the architecture we so much enjoy today.

82. The south side of the extended Pump Room overlooking the King's Bath is shown in J. Ryall's print of 1764 which gives a good impression of the heavily built up nature of the surroundings.

As the facilities of the city improved so the pattern of its social life changed. In the late seventeenth century the season had been short: Bath was a town 'where all the people live all the winter (like nightingales) upon the stock of their summer fat' but gradually throughout the early eighteenth century the single summer season became two, one in autumn and one in spring. By 1762 they had coalesced into a single six months extending through the winter, and twenty years later the contemporary Bath guides warn that the expensive months begin in September and last until May.

People came in increasing numbers. The *Bath Journal* listed annually the number of persons of distinction visiting the city: in 1746 it was 510, by 1800 it had increased tenfold to 5341. But those worthy to be noted were only a small fraction of the actual visitor numbers. According to John Wood, writing in 1749, there was even then accommodation for some 12,000. The economy of the city was now entirely dependent upon the tourist trade, the majority of its citizens providing the considerable range of goods and services that such a colossal influx not only demanded but could also well afford.

83.   Rowlandson's wicked evocation offers a different view of deportment in the King's Bath in 1798.

But the eighteenth century was not one long romp for the rich and elegant. The very popularity of the place attracted the lower classes – the mere gentry – in increasing numbers and as the exclusive nature of the resort was diluted so the aristocracy began to lose interest. This was now the Bath about which Smollett and Sheridan wrote. Smollett's wickedly sharp tongue, communicating to us through the voice of his character Matthew Bramble (in *Humphrey Clinker*), gives a brilliant picture of the *nouveau riche* now invading the spa. 'Every upstart of fortune, harnessed in the trappings of the mode, presents himself at Bath, as the very focus of observation. Clerks and factors from the East Indies, loaded with the spoil of plundered provinces, planters, negro drivers, and hucksters from our American plantations, enriched they know not how, agents, commissaries, and contractors, who have fattened, in two successive wars, on the blood of the nation; usurers, brokers, and jobbers of every kind; men of low birth and no breeding, have found themselves suddenly translated into a state of affluence, unknown to former ages; and no wonder that their brows should be intoxicated with pride, vanity and presumptuousness . . . and all of them hurrying to Bath, because here, without any further qualification, they can mingle with the princes and nobles of the land'.

This cruel but evocative tirade (and there is much more of it) was written in 1771, the year in which the Assembly Rooms were completed and the Royal Crescent was emerging new-built from its scaffolding. Smollett's 'uncouth whales of fortune' as he calls them, were able to swim in an ornate aquarium.

Bath's gradual loss of appeal was born of many factors: the enacting of new anti-gambling laws, the lack of a charismatic master of ceremonies, the changing fortunes of the old nobility and the great influx of new men – these all took their toll, but in many ways the death knell was sounded when Bath began to attract not visitors, but new residents – retired civil servants, superannuated parsons and army officers on half pay. In short, even before the end of the eighteenth century, Bath had begun to slip inevitably into its new role as a retirement town. The places of public assembly were now no longer fashionable: 'evening amusements were solely in the elegant stupidity of private parties' Jane Austen tells us. But it is in *Northanger Abbey* that she gives her most damning indictment of the city she found so dull. Bath was where her character Sir Walter Elliot, an impoverished member of the Somerset gentry, chose to live. It was, she said, 'a much safer place for a gentleman in his predicament: he might there be important at comparatively little expense'.

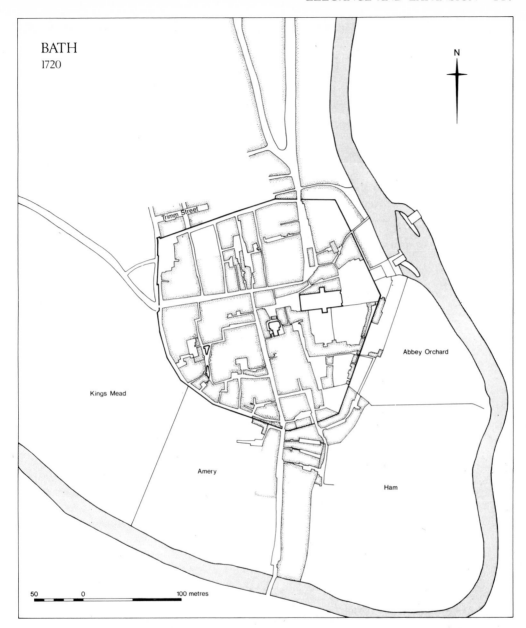

BATH
1720

N

Trimm Street

Kings Mead

Amery

Abbey Orchard

Ham

50   0   100 metres

84.   Bath in *c.* 1720 was still largely constrained by the medieval walls and the medieval street pattern. Outside were the two medieval suburbs and the beginnings of the eighteenth century expansion, Trim Street to the north and Orchard Street to the south-east. The plan is based on an estate map of 1725. (Source: author).

To understand how Bath grew in the eighteenth century we must say something of the ownership of land and of the entrepreneurial attitudes that were now in the air. Much of the land within the old walled city and several large tracts outside belonged to the Corporation and they managed it, as landlord, for the corporate good. They also had control of the town's commons occupying the slope of Lansdown to the west of the city. For the first half of the century the Corporation was a cautious landlord choosing to maintain the terms of the hundreds of small lease holds, into which the urban core was divided, rather than to initiate new building schemes. Indeed the only significant innovation was the successful soliciting leading to the Turnpike and Improvement Act of 1707 which allowed a system of turnpikes to be established on the roads leading into Bath. Ancillary clauses provided for the cleaning, paving and lighting of the streets and for the organization of chairmen. Here was the Corporation maintaining its assets.

But there were in and immediately around Bath large areas in private ownership. Much of the priory land had eventually passed into the hands of the Duke of Kingston; the considerable area of Barton Farm, to the west of the walled city, between it and the common, belonged to Dr. Robert Gay, a London surgeon, while Kingsmead to the south, down to the River Avon, was in the possession of Lovelace Haynes, an absentee landlord who lived in Berkshire. These agrarian capitalists were interested in maximizing on their assets and as soon as pressure for suitable building land, in close proximity to the urban core, increased, they and their like were quickly persuaded to reparcel their holdings and disperse them on long profitable leases to the speculators and builders eager to try their luck in the exciting markets which Bath was now providing.

John Wood the elder, Bath's most famous architect, understood the market well. His system was very simple. He would lease a plot of land from its owner, subdivide it into house-sized plots which he would then sublease to builders. Imposed upon the area was one of Wood's great overall architectural schemes. He planned the streets and designed the facades and as developer he also had to prepare the site – to lay it out and provide the water and sewage systems. It was then up to the individual builders, using mortgage money they had raised, and under Wood's overall supervision of the facades, to build what houses they wished. In this way much of Georgian Bath was born.

The Corporation steered well clear of such speculative ventures for half a century, but by 1750 they could resist no longer, and entered with enthusiasm into the redevelopment of the Town Acre which lay to the north of the walled city. One of the outcomes of this was Milsom Street which was begun in 1763. The same decade also saw the demolition and redevelopment of much of the old city wall, now regarded as a hindrance to progress. Westgate Buildings was to emerge on the newly-created space. With the bit now well between their teeth, the Corporation turned to the ancient urban core intent at last to thoroughly modernize it. The City Act of 1766 and the Improvement Act of 1789 provided the necessary legal framework and the Lower Town was impressively redesigned. The last of the great buildings – the Pump Room – was eventually completed in 1796 just in time to witness the final stages of Bath's decline as a fashionable spa.

Against this general background, so briefly sketched, we can now return to the fabric of the city to trace its century of spectacular growth.

The first 25 years of the eighteenth century was a prelude but by no means an uneventful one. Oliver Goldsmith, writing of the Bath when Beau Nash arrived in 1702, leaves us in no doubt of the town's dowdiness. 'The lodgings for visitors were paltry though expensive: the dining-rooms and other chambers were floored with boards, coloured brown with soot and small-beer, to hide the dirt; the walls were covered with unpainted wainscot; the furniture corresponded with the meanness of the archi-tecture; a few oak chairs, a small looking-glass, with a fender and tongs, composed the magnificence of these temporary habitations. The city was in itself mean and contemptible; no elegant buildings, no open streets, nor uniform squares!'.

It was not long before the entrepreneurs were at work. The first of these was George Trymme, a gentleman clothier and member of the Corporation. He owned a small plot of land just outside the north wall and in 1707 he breached the city wall and laid out a short street (Trim Street) leasing off plots of land to speculative builders. His example was soon followed by Richard Marchant, a member of the Company of Merchant Taylors. In 1709 he purchased the lease on a plot of land on the edge of the Hams, just outside the south-eastern wall and proceeded to lay out streets (Marchant's Passage) and courts and to build a number of houses. A third extramural development took place in 1719 just outside the West gate where John Thornburgh put up several new houses of quality. Together these three men, speculators relying heavily on other men's money, set the scene for what was soon to follow.

Meanwhile, within the town the Corporation had not been

idle. The needs of the visitors were being looked after. The habit of drinking the spring water was by now well established, but the facilities to indulge it were of the most primitive outdoor kind. Spurred on by the famous Dr. Oliver and a number of other leading physicians, the Corporation agreed to build a Pump Room on a plot of land immediately adjacent to the north side of the King's Bath. It was completed in 1706 by a local builder, John Harvey, and to judge from contemporary illustrations was a charming single-storey structure built in the style of an orangery (ill. 80). It had four large openings on the north and south sides, 'These large Apertures are filled up with Sashes and Sash Doors; and a Gallery projects out of the Wall at the West End of the Room, sufficient to hold a small Band of Musick for the Entertainment of the Water Drinkers every Morning during the seasons' (John Wood). This elegant little structure was a considerable addition to Bath's meagre stock of good architecture.

Not far away, just to the east of the abbey church, Nash persuaded a local man, Thomas Harrison, to build an Assembly Room on the line of the old city wall between Terrace Walk and the river (ill. 94). Harrison's Rooms were an immediate success and the original structure, consisting of a card room and a tea-room, was soon extended to include a ballroom built in 1720. Nor were the outdoor needs of the visitor overlooked. Harrison himself laid out walks behind his Assembly Rooms on the edge of Abbey Orchard, while close by the Gravel Walks and

85.   One of the elegant public areas of early eighteenth century Bath was the Orange Grove which lay between the east end of the abbey and the city wall. It was named after the obelisk erected in honour of William of Orange.

Orange Grove were created in an area of semi-derelict land east of the abbey which had once been the site of the quire and north transept of the Norman cathedral priory (ill. 81). Nash took a considerable personal interest in the work and when it was proposed to close the south side of the Orange Grove with a terrace of houses, he insisted that 'a handsome pavement was then made for the company to walk on'. The terrace, in a refaced guise, and the pavement still survive looking out across the square which had once been the Orange Grove, and is now sadly reduced to a monstrous traffic roundabout, taxi rank and bus terminal (ills. 85 and 86).

The first twenty-five years of the century saw, then, a mild flurry of activity within the old walled area, designed to improve, in a modest way, the facilities provided for visitors. Compared to the Assembly Rooms to be built in the Upper Town between 1768 and 1771, and the Grand Pump Room completed in 1796, their predecessors were modest indeed, but it was a beginning. Much the same can be said of the speculative housing ventures of Marchant, Trymme and Thornburgh: nonetheless in these early schemes a system of credit and finance had been created which was to be followed with spectacular results by the Woods and their successors.

86.   The area of the Orange Grove is now a noisy traffic roundabout redolent with petrol fumes but could so easily be restored to its former peace given vision and strength of purpose. The facades of the buildings on the south side were regularized by Major Davis in the 1890s.

In 1725 the architect John Wood heard news of a scheme to improve the navigation of the Avon between Bristol and Bath. And so began the adventure that was to transform Bath from a cramped rather scruffy town into one of the most beautiful cities in the world. 'When I found Work was likely to go on, I began to turn my Thoughts towards the Improvement of the City by Building; and for the Purpose I procured a Plan of the Town, which was sent me into Yorkshire, in the Summer of the Year 1725, where I, at my leisure Hours, formed one Design for the Ground, at the North West Corner of the City; and another for the Land, on the North East Side of the Town and River'. He then goes on to outline his grand scheme, 'in each Design, I proposed to make a grand Place of Assembly, to be called the Royal Forum of Bath; another Place, no less magnificent, for the exhibition of Sports, to be called the Grand Circus; and a third Place, of equal State with either of the former, for the Practice of medicinal Exercises, to be called the Imperial Gymnasium of the City, from a Work of that Kind, taking its Rise at first in Bath, during the Time of the Roman Emperors'. The sheer audacity of the scheme and the arrogance of its perpetrator is staggering. Here on the hill slopes, around the old medieval core of Bath, Wood was proposing to create a new Rome suited to the manners and susceptibilities of his time – a great Palladian city.

Vision is one thing: the practicalities of speculative building quite another and negotiations for suitable land in Barton Farm dragged on. Meanwhile Wood found other jobs in the city. He completed the rebuilding of St. John's Hospital for the Duke of Chandos in 1727, and the next year designed a new Assembly Room, known as Lindsey's Rooms, on Terrace Walk opposite Harrison's Rooms. At last, the leases drawn up, on 10 December, 1728 the foundations were dug for his first, and probably his greatest creation – Queen's Square – set in a corner of Barton fields between the Bristol Road and the town lands backing onto the Broad Street properties (ill. 88). Wood created an architectural composition quite unlike anything that the city had known – it was a development of private houses, unified behind a series of Palladian facades forming a single architectural concept, the whole dominated by the palace-like front of the northern range. Everything about the design reflects the restraint, balance and harmony inherent in Palladian proportions. Even the open space, the square itself and its parades, echo the order. As Wood explains, 'the Intention of a Square in a City is for People to assemble together; and the Spot whereon they meet, ought to be separated from the Ground

common to Men and Beasts, and even to Mankind in General, if Decency and good order are necessary to be observed in such Places of Assembly; of which, I think, there can be no doubt'. Here, then, was design in harmony with genteel function.

Queen's Square, began in 1728 and finished in 1735, was the most spectacular of two developments lying to the west of the

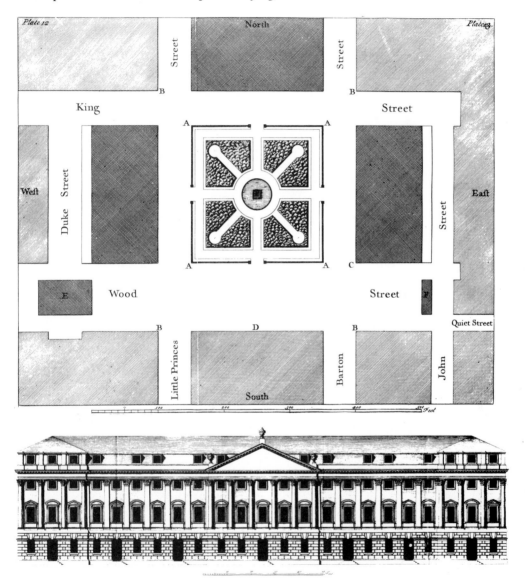

87 and 88. John Wood's first major addition to Bath was Queen's Square built between 1728 and 1735. Wood's original scheme (ill. 87) was slightly modified in reality. The strength of the concept lay in the quality of its uniform facades (ill. 88).

89 and 90.   T. Malton's aquatint of Queen's Square 1784 catches the atmosphere of spacious tranquility (ill. 89). Contrast with the same view today (ill. 90).

city. The second, immediately outside West gate, consisted of
two squares, Kingsmead Square and Beaufort Buildings and
three streets, Kingsmead Street, Monmouth Street (the original
Bristol Road) and Avon Street. The leasehold of Kingsmead
land at this stage had been acquired by a Bristol timber
merchant, John Hobbs, and it was he who was masterminding
the Avon navigation scheme. Hobbs had employed for this a
Bristol architect, John Strahan, in preference to John Wood, and
continued to employ Strahan when, in 1727, the Kingsmead
development began. The work was small-scale and completely
unostentatious and as such earned Wood's scathing criticism,
more vitriolic than usual because he saw Strahan as a rival. It
did, nonetheless, contain buildings of quality, like the delightful
baroque Rosewell House built in 1736 (ill. 91) and the
constrained houses of Beaufort Square, but the development
did not, nor was it intended to, compete with the affluent
elegance of Wood's creation. Avon Street is particularly interesting. It was laid out as a means of access to New Quay on the
Avon bank, and from the beginning was conceived of as lower
middle class accommodation. Its unhealthy location, on the
Avon flood plain, and the incessant traffic to and from the river
quay, quickly made it unappealing, and by the middle of the
century its decline is detectable. By the Victorian era it had

91. Rosewell House in
Kingsmead Square was
probably designed by
John Strahan in 1736 as
part of the Kingsmead
development for which
he was responsible. The
Baroque style, unique in
Bath, was considered of
little interest and the
building was threatened
with demolition.
Fortunately (though
mutilated by shop fronts)
it is now safe and
cherished.

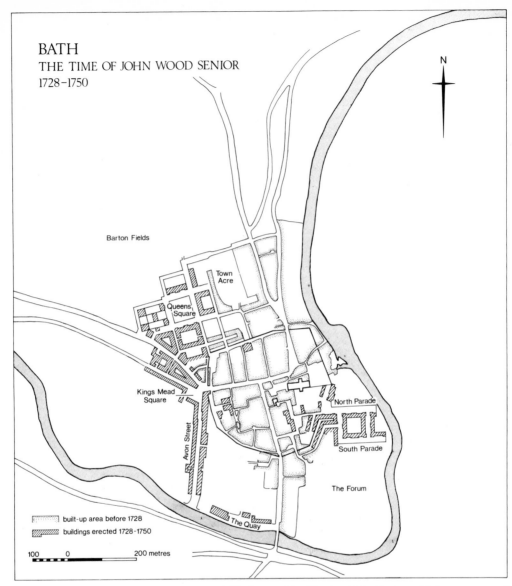

BATH
THE TIME OF JOHN WOOD SENIOR
1728-1750

N

Barton Fields

Town
Acre

Queens
Square

Kings Mead
Square

North Parade

Avon Street

South Parade

The Forum

built-up area before 1728
buildings erected 1728-1750

The Quay

100   0   200 metres

92.   Bath in the period 1728–50 began to expand. To the west John Wood and John Strahan added new streets and
squares, the Upper Bristol Road roughly dividing the work of the two rivals. To the east John Wood began a grandiose
scheme with his North and South Parades. (Source: author).

become the most squalid and notorious street of Bath's depressed southern area, the resort of robbers and prostitutes: the nymphs of Avon Street were rarely mentioned in polite company.

Bath continued to be a city with a conscience. Alongside the aristocratic visitors who came mainly to enjoy the life style and to see and be seen was a constant stream of poor, destitute and sick. The philanthropic institutions set up in the sixteenth century were no longer able to cope, so in 1716 a group of local dignitaries came together to begin to raise funds for a new free hospital to care for 'poor lepers, cripples and other indigent persons resorting to Bath for a cure . . . and to discriminate real objects of charity from vagrants and other imposters who crowd both the church and the town to the annoyance of the gentry resorting there'. The scheme's sponsors and benefactors included Dr. William Oliver and Beau Nash. The wealthy local business man, Ralph Allan, provided all the stone free from his quarries while Wood donated his services as an architect. The hospital – known for much of its life as the Mineral Water Hospital – was completed between 1738 and 1742. It stood (and still does but with later modifications) on a rather restricted site in Upper Borough Walls which had previously been occupied by the old theatre. From here the inmates could hobble, largely out of sight, down Vicarage Lane and Cross Bath Lane, to take free treatment at the Hot Bath, thus giving little 'annoyance' to the 'gentry' whose social life focused on the Pump Room, the two Assembly Rooms and the Gravel Walks, amenities which were now conveniently linked by a short cut, Wade's Passage, slicing the old buildings north of the abbey church.

Wood's Queen's Square development was inconveniently distant from the social focus and it was largely for this reason that he now turned his attention on the Abbey Orchard – an area of marshy ground on the east side of town between the city wall and the River Avon (ill. 93). It was here he had intended to build his Circus, but the grand scheme was altered 'to a Forum to extend southwards to the South Part of Ham, as a Place of publick Assembly'. In the simplicity of Wood's scheme lay its magnificence. Across the low-lying orchard he thrust out a massive raised platform supported on vaults and on this created two great facades fronting a number of individual houses. Each looked out across a parade to an open area beyond; the northern front, across Grand (later North) Parade to St. James triangle, the southern, across South Parade to the Royal Forum. Access between the two parades was provided by two wide cross streets, Duke Street and Pierrepoint Street.

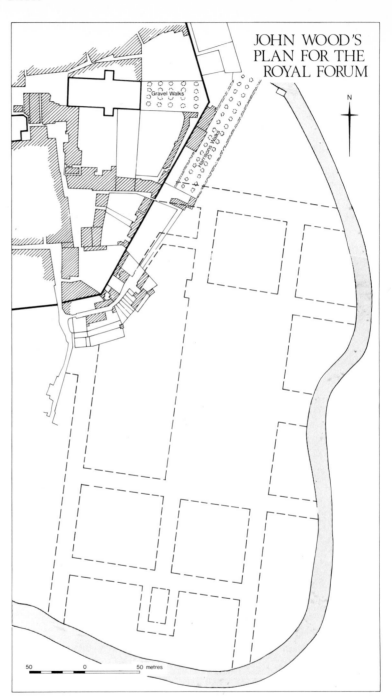

JOHN WOOD'S
PLAN FOR THE
ROYAL FORUM

Gravel Walks

N

93. John Wood senior proposed a major development to the east of the city covering the Abbey Orchard and the Hams. The plan, based on a manuscript plan of 1725, gives some idea of his grand scheme which was to include a Royal Forum. (Source: author).

50   0   50 metres

The Abbey Orchard development was to provide everything that the elegant visitor could wish, spacious accommodation set within a unified architectural scheme, magnificent outlooks and ease of access to the social heart of Bath. Wood even proposed to build a new suite of assembly rooms within the Royal Forum. Work began in 1739 and within nine years had been completed to a modified plan. The facades were less grand than Wood had intended and the idea of the forum had to be totally abandoned, but even so what was achieved was a splendid harmonious addition to Bath's facilities. Today the buildings remain, the integrity of their design spoilt by a clutter of hotel and restaurant signs (ill. 96). North Parade is now a main exit road from the city centre but the worst disaster lies to the south. Where the Great Forum was to be, a potentially magnificent open space with quite spectacular views to the hills beyond, there is now an eclectic jumble of structures including churches, a police station, modern office blocks, a garage and a two-storey car park. The kindest thing that can be said is that as individual buildings they have little merit; as an example of urban planning it is a disaster.

In 1754, the year of his death, Wood began his third great design – the Circus (ill. 98). His plan for rebuilding the city centre had been rejected by the Corporation so he turned once more to the Barton fields to add one final touch of brilliance to

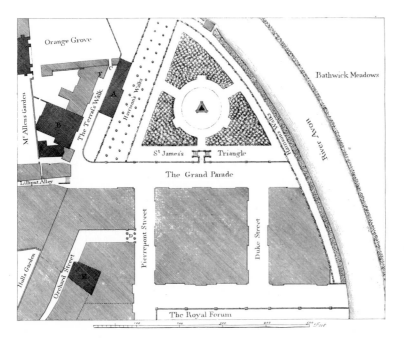

94. John Wood senior's own plan of the North and South Parades, as they were built, shows how little of his grand scheme (ill. 93) was actually accomplished.

95 and 96. Duffield's view of South Parade *c.* 1830 contrasts with South Parade today.

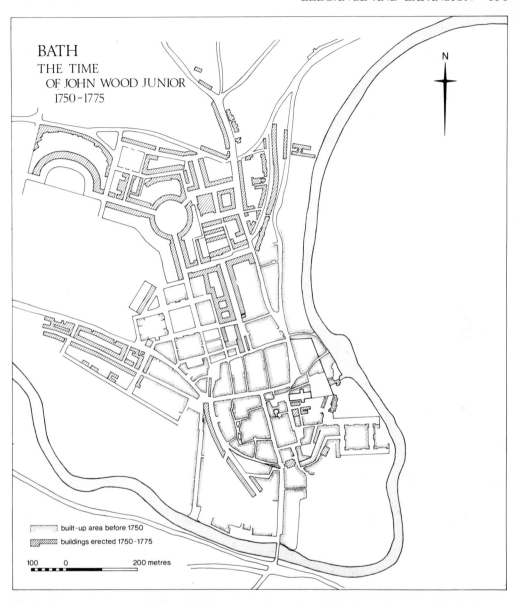

BATH
THE TIME
OF JOHN WOOD JUNIOR
1750–1775

N

built-up area before 1750
buildings erected 1750–1775

100   0   200 metres

97.   Bath's expansion between 1750 and 1775 was largely the creation of John Wood the younger. His father's plan for the Circus and his own for the Royal Crescent provided the heart of the Upper Town. (Source: author).

the Bath he had largely recreated. The Circus is a masterpiece. Entirely inward looking it is an essay in triplism: three streets approach it, dividing the circle of buildings into three great arcs, while the facades themselves are composed of three horizontal tiers one upon the other. Today with its central garden and mature trees, enlivened by on-street parking, the Circus sometimes feels a little oppressive and visually over-busy, but in its original state, paved across without interruption, the feeling of controlled space, the light, and the fresh air of the upper city, would have made it a place without parallel – urban perfection thrust into the heart of the countryside.

Wood did not live to see his dream realized but the Circus was completed according to his designs by his son John Wood the younger in 1758 – a year which marks the beginning of a short pause in Bath's expansion.

Throughout much of this first period of urban growth, 1725–1758, the city Corporation sat back and watched. It was not entirely inactive: the Pump Room was extended in 1752, but the Corporation did not begin to dabble in serious building speculation until 1755 when it developed a strip of land on the southern side of London Road, allowing to be erected a long terrace of houses called Bladud Buildings. The range is particularly interesting for having both front and back treated as a unified facade by an unknown architect.

It was also at this time that there began negotiations with Daniel Milsom, granting him a lease on a block of land, including the Town Acre to the north of George Street, which runs between Broad Street and Wood's Queen's Square development. This paved the way for the creation of Milsom Street a few years later which allowed the long strip of gardens, extending northwards from the city wall, and now largely isolated between the ancient Broad Street development and Wood's Upper Town, to be developed as a main thoroughfare.

The problem of communications was certainly exercising the attention of the Corporation at this time. The old city was still surrounded by its city wall and the narrow medieval gates were a considerable impediment. But in 1754 the Corporation acted. The south gate was removed first, followed by the North gate. The *Bath Journal* of 3 March, 1755 records approvingly, 'Last week the North Gate of the city was pulled down, as well as the Houses on each side, in order to make that avenue more commodious which before was very narrow .... The late and useful and great alterations made in the widening of the bridge, the making of avenues leading to the city more convenient for passengers etc., etc., must rebound on the Honor of the present

98 and 99.   The Circus, planned by John Wood senior was built by his son between 1754 and 1770. It is a masterpiece. Conceived of as a vast open space (as in this etching of 1773) it was soon cluttered with trees (planted 1790) and, more recently, with traffic.

members of the Corporation to latest posterity'. Not until 1776 was the West gate removed.

In the thirty years or so of Bath's first great expansion much of the town had been transformed but the vast open areas and yard upon yard of stark modern facade were not to everyone's liking. As early as 1736 Jonathan Swift was writing, 'This town has grown to such an enormous size that above half the day must be spent in the streets in going from one place to another. I like it every year less and less'. And in 1779 the author of a satire, *Bath – a Simile*, likened the architecture of the Upper Town to a monstrous tea service matched in fashionable triviality only by the incessant rounds of mindless tea-drinking indulged in by its occupants.

Before the Circus was completed the market slumped as Britain plunged into the Seven Years War and for a while speculative building ceased, but it was soon to pick up again to herald Bath's second great period of expansion – 1762–74. 'A rage of building' was how Smollett described the city in 1763. The results were spectacular (ill. 97): from the edge of the common, where the younger Wood had sited his Royal Crescent, the Upper Town spread in a great arc of streets and terraces around the lower slopes of Lansdown, creeping out into the countryside to the east along the London Road. Kingsmead, to the south-west of the city, was completely built up with terraces of modest houses for the working and lower middle classes, while building of the same kind extended westwards along Kingsmead Street and Monmouth Street. To the east expansion was halted by the river, but in 1769–74 Pulteney Bridge was built by Sir Richard Pulteney as the first step in the development of his Bathwick estate which was soon to follow.

Much of the expansion of the Upper Town was the work of John Wood the younger. The crowning glory of his prodigious output was the Royal Crescent, set at arm's length from the Circus (ill. 100): Brock Street which joins them was deliberately contrived to be a calming influence between the great sensations at either end. The Crescent fully deserves its reputation of being perhaps the most perfect essay in urban architecture in the western world, but it should not be allowed to detract from Wood's main achievement of blending together his and his father's individual designs into a single urban whole complete in itself, breath taking in its variety and totally without precedent or parallel. The Upper Town, as it was known, was Wood's creation: those who followed merely added to it.

The emergence of the Upper Town created a tension: Bath had become a town with two centres pulling against each other.

100 and 101.   John Wood junior built the Royal Crescent between 1767 and 1775. The sheer size and audacity of the scheme, thrust on to a green hillside beyond the edge of the city, must have shocked. Cozen's aquatint of 1773 captures the mood (ill. 100). Even today little has changed. Rowlandson's concept emphasizes some aspects of the location (ill. 101)

Downtown Bath – the Lower Town – was old-fashioned and cramped, its atmosphere often hot and enervating. It had little to offer other than its baths and when, in 1771, Wood's New Assembly Rooms were completed just behind the Circus the balance tipped even further against the old centre. In the Lower Town one set of Rooms closed immediately; the other struggled.

Ever mindful of its tourist income, the Corporation began to consider large-scale renovations. The Hot Baths were by now ripe for redevelopment and the contract for complete rebuilding was given to Wood who, between 1773–7, produced an exquisite little structure, perfectly designed to provide private covered bathing for the select few (ill. 102). It was a marked advance on the open public pools which the city had inherited from its medieval past and was to set new standards for the next phase of spa development a century later. It was also the beginning of a new civic awareness that was to be a feature of the third period of expansion.

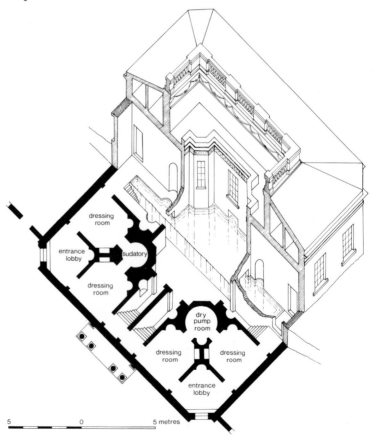

102.   Renovation of the bathing facilities came comparatively late. The first significant improvement was to the Hot Bath which was completely rebuilt as a semi-enclosed pool by John Wood the younger 1775–78. His solution to the problem of providing some privacy for the bathers was adopted by Baldwin at the King's Bath ten years later. Wood's building still survives though heavily modifed. (Source: author after John Wood).

The quite remarkable achievements of the younger Wood completely overshadow the other architect-builders at work in Bath at the time, but two must be mentioned. Thomas Warr Atwood, a wealthy plumber glazier, became city architect during this period. It was he who extended the Corporation's development along London Road by adding the gentle sweep of Paragon Buildings to the earlier, more limited, development of Bladud Buildings. His involvement in speculative schemes was long, complex, and probably corrupt, but he was evidently a man of some originality whose abilities were suddenly terminated when the floor of an old house fell and killed him in 1775. The second architect of this period was Robert Adam, the only outsider to make his mark on Bath. As a friend of Sir William Pulteney he was the obvious man to choose when Pulteney decided to develop his Bathwick estate on the east bank of the Avon. A bridge joining the new development to the old city was an essential prerequisite and Adam's response to the challenge was brilliantly inventive and elegant in the extreme (ill. 103). Work commenced in 1769 and was completed in 1774. The bridge was to be only a beginning and indeed Adam prepared two designs for the proposed Bathwick estate (ill. 106) but Pulteney's death and the temporary collapse of the market during the war years led to the scheme being shelved for the time being.

Building projects in Bath suffered generally during the war. As one local surveyor wrote a few years later, 'from the year

103.   By the late eighteenth century Bath had grown to such an extent that the prospect of further expansion across the river in Bathwick was seriously considered. William Johnstone-Pulteney commissioned Robert Adam to build a new bridge and to prepare designs for the layout of the estate. In the event only the bridge was built to Adam's designs (1769–74)

104 and 105.   J.C. Nattes' aquatint shows the scene in 1805 from North Parade. The same view today dominated by monsters – the Empire Hotel and Beaufort Hotel.

1778 to the year 1783 by reason of our dispute with America, our army and navy being then on service, the seasons at Bath were so little frequented that houses in Bath were greatly reduced in value'. But once the war, and the concurrent financial crisis, were over, Bath was gripped by another building boom: restricted to a brief decade – 1783–93 – it was the third and last of the city's spectacular advances. In a final surge uphill the Upper Town spread from Wood's core higher and higher up the slopes of Lansdown. John Palmer added St. James's Square and Lansdown Crescent between 1789 and 1793; John Eveleigh built Camden Place (1788) and Somerset Place (*c.* 1790) and there were a number of other lesser developments providing for the first time less expensive houses in an area of higher density building in the streets between Cottes Lane and Lansdown Road. And out along the London Road the speculators advanced, throwing up terraces: Kensington Place put up by John Palmer in 1795, Percy Place and Alexander Buildings, culminating in John Eveleigh's Grosvenor Place (1791) beyond which lay the open countryside again. From Marlborough Buildings just west of the Royal Crescent to Grosvenor Place the eighteenth century terraces spread in a continuous ever-changing ribbon for nearly a mile and a quarter!

Meanwhile to the east, the development of the Bathwick estate was gradually getting underway – not Adam's scheme but according to the plans drawn up by Thomas Baldwin (ill. 107). The main axis of Laura Place and Great Pulteney Street was laid out and built between 1788 and 1790 together with part of Bathwick Street. Henrietta Street, which was to lead to the huge Frances Square, the centre of the development, was finished, but there the project halted. The French Revolution caused shock waves to run through the financial markets, banks collapsed and what was to be Bath's greatest speculative development shuddered to a halt forcing builders and developers, like Eveleigh and Baldwin, into bankruptcy. Today Pulteney Street has an air of unreality: it is stage-set thin – little more than a facade joining Pulteney Bridge and Laura Place to the fine hexagonal expanse of Sydney Gardens – and it exudes the insubstantial feeling of the unfinished. Had Baldwin's finances not collapsed the fully developed Bathwick estate would undoubtedly have shown him to have been a town planner of unusual vision and skill.

Further extensions to the city were also made to the south-west into the previously open area of Great Kingsmead. Kingsmead Terrace (1792) was followed by the beginning of the Green Park development (1799 completed 1808) but the region

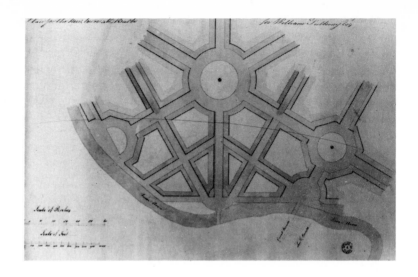

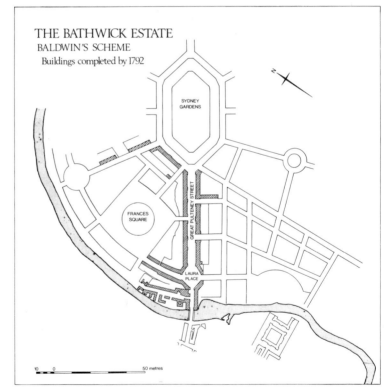

106 and 107. Robert Adam's plans for the layout of Bathwick estate survived but were never followed (above). Thomas Baldwin modified the designs but by the end of the century only the main axis of Laura Place, Pulteney Street and Sydney Gardens had been completed (ill. below). Thereafter development was piecemeal and bore little resemblance to the original schemes. (Source of ill. 107: author).

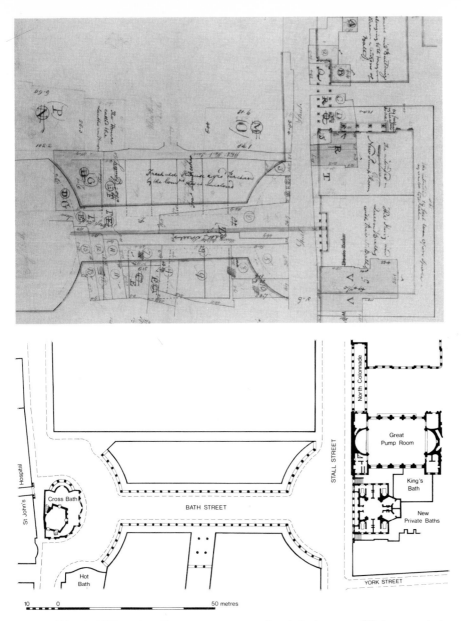

108 and 109.   In 1788 a series of improvements were put in train in the centre of Bath to upgrade the baths and make the communications between them more efficient. Plans were drawn up by Thomas Baldwin and entailed extensive widening and realignment of streets. A major element in Baldwin's scheme was the creation of Bath Street and the complete refurnishment of the King's Bath complex involving the construction of the New Private Baths (1788) and the North Colonnade (1786) and the Great Pump Room, (begun in 1790). The manuscript plan (ill. 108) shows the property changes necessary. The final scheme (ill. 109) was completed by 1800. The Pump Room, as originally planned, was to have a projectiong portico; when finished by Palmer the portico was much reduced, spoiling the proportions. (Source of ill. 109: author after Isons 1948, fig. 5).

was never regarded as particularly salubrious and large open areas remained.

It was during this third period that the city Corporation finally grasped the problem of the inconvenient and antiquated city core. As early as 1752 Smollett had written, 'The Corporation of Bath seems to have forgot that the ease and plenty they now enjoy, and to which their fathers were strangers, are owing to their waters; and that an improvement upon their baths would, by bringing a greater concourse of company to their town, perpetuate these blessings to them and their posterity'. But in 1766 the City Act was passed which gave the Corporation powers to move the market place, enlarge the Pump Room, improve the baths and enter into compulsory purchase contracts as were necessary. Even so things got off to a very uncertain start: clearing the market place was easy enough but the rebuilding of the Guildhall involved the Corporation in interminable wrangles which were to last for many years and it was not until 1777 that the building was completed according to the plans of Thomas Baldwin (ill. 111). The next year Wood completed his rebuilding of the Hot Bath; the Cross Bath was modified in 1784 and the years following. But still the central problem of the narrow inconvenient streets and the dismal state of the King's and Queen's Baths had not been faced.

Eventually a council committee was set up to consider what improvements were necessary: it reported, 'That the most eligible method of doing it is by making very convenient thoroughfares through the city; which can only be done by widening some of the old streets, making an open communication between the Upper and Lower Town and laying the Baths as open as possible, to complete which, Mr. Baldwin is desired to draw an accurate plan of the city, describing where such improvements are most necessary to be made'. Baldwin's plan was finally submitted in March 1788 and accepted by the council (ill. 108). The necessary act of parliament – the Improvement Act – was passed in June 1789.

The plan involved the complete rebuilding of the Pump Room and King's Bath complex and the creation of five new streets. Bath Street, Beau Street, Hot Bath Street and Nash Street were designed to improve communications between the baths while Union Street was to link Milsom Street and the Upper Town direct to Stall Street and the baths. That the entire project, except for the completion of Nash Street, was achieved says much for the Corporation's determination.

Even before the Act was passed work had begun on the Pump Room/King's Bath complex (ill. 107). In 1786 Baldwin had

110.   The Pump Room was eventually finished in 1796 by John Palmer. The south front viewed in 1801 shows the grandeur of Baldwin's scheme.

111.   Thomas Baldwin's Bath masterpiece is the Guildhall built in 1776 seen here in a steel engraving of 1839. Even now, with John McKean Brydon's additions of 1891, the quality of the building can still be appreciated.

built a gentle, restrained colonnade across the approaches to Abbey Churchyard just north of the old Pump Room, and two years later he completed the New Private Baths to the south, its facade neatly echoing that of the north colonnade. The baths followed, in concept at least, the Hot Baths of John Wood: they provided enclosed and private bathing facilities – six suites, each comprising a bath and a dressing room – opening from a central rotunda. Both elements were clearly designed as part of the same unified scheme which was to have the monolithic mass of the Great Pump Room between.

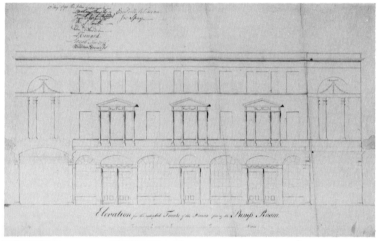

112 and 113. As part of the redevelopment scheme nearby buildings were cut back and refaced. Baldwin's schemes for those facing the main front of the Pump Room were restrained and elegant (ill. 112). The unity of Baldwin's schemes have been ruined by modern shop fronts (ill. 113).

Eventually in the autumn of 1790 work began digging the foundations of the new Pump Room. The next year while building work was progressing slowly the new line of Bath Street was sliced through a maze of old buildings and lanes giving direct access between the Cross Bath and New Private Baths. The street was lined with continuous colonnades and at each end opened out into a wide colonnaded hemicycle. It was a brilliant piece of planning and can be enjoyed today, even though the view from the Cross Bath is marred by the totally inappropriate Victorian fountain that stands, vulgar and askew, obscuring the front of the New Private Baths.

Work on the Pump Room was slow and after a violent disagreement with the Corporation Baldwin was eventually dismissed; the next year he was bankrupt. John Palmer took over but it was not until 1796 that the interior was finally completed.

The city centre improvements had been far more costly than the Corporation had anticipated. The war with France and the depression of 1793 meant that it had become increasingly difficult to sell leases to local builders. Building programmes staggered to a halt and the Grand Pump Room opened its doors to the public in an atmosphere of gloom. The last remnants of the Improvement scheme – the creation of Union Street and York Street – were delayed until the beginning of the nineteenth century.

The crash of 1793 thrust Bath into depression: banks broke and builders toppled as one speculative venture after another ran out of capital and failed to attract new investment. But it was more than that: it marked a turning point in Bath's fortunes. The city had grown too fast, it was too big. No longer could it claim to be an exclusive resort. The trendsetters were looking elsewhere, to Cheltenham or to the newly discovered delights of sea bathing at Brighton and Weymouth. Eighteenth century Bath had been born of a social demand effectively served by enthusiastic capitalism. What emerged was magnificent, but a magnificence on so grand and uncontrolled a scale that it stifled the original charm of the place: its greatness was the cause of its collapse. In the early years of the nineteenth century the fringes of the huge urban sprawl were to thrust a little further into the countryside but Bath – the high watermark of eighteenth century urban splendour – was now left high and dry by the fast receding tide of fashion.

But we cannot leave the Georgian city on a down beat. Standing back from it all one staggering realization remains: the magnificence we now rate so highly was all, virtually without exception, created in the space of only 70 years – by local men.

7. THE SEARCH FOR IDENTITY: 1800–1940

FOR 150 YEARS, from the economic collapse of 1793 to the end of the Second World War, the story of Bath was the story of a city in decline – a city in search of an identity. The honey-coloured freshness of its genteel facades soon faded. Drabness crept over the face of the city as black grime began to crust its every building. The sedan chair gave way to the bath chair but even they eventually disappeared. A 'grass grown city of the ancients' was how Dickens described it. Yet there was always hope of a great revival. Many pinned their faith on the opening of the railway in 1841, but little came of it. The city authorities made a monumental effort in the 1870s–80s to revitalize the spa using all the trappings of contemporary technology but the world was not impressed and so, with little to enliven or sustain it, Bath lapsed into provincial lethargy.

Why then bother too much with the period? The answer is that we are interested in the trajectory of Bath's urban development: only by watching it change through time, deflected by the influences of events, will we be able to understand the organic nature of a city. Eighteenth century Bath shot forward with an amazing self-generating energy. For the next 150 years, its force largely spent, the city struggled to cope with its legacy. That story of struggle has a fascination of its own. It too has imposed structure on the landscape – a structure with which present generations have to contend.

The depression of the 1790s shook the building industry. Many developer-architects went bankrupt, projects ground to a halt and terraces stood unfinished. One victim of the times was John Pinch, a builder, whose bankruptcy was announced soon after 1800. But Pinch was a man of energy and ability and by 1807 we find him in business again as a surveyor and architect, designing in a late eighteenth century mode around the northern and western fringes of the city, most successfully at New Sydney Place (1807–8), Park Street (1808), Cavendish Place (1808–17), Cavendish Crescent (1817–30) and Sion Hill Place (1817–20). His work is essentially the last expression of the grand urban-Palladian tradition – fine in detail and balance but intensely conservative in style.

John Pinch's death in 1827 marks the end of an era but already styles were beginning to change. Pinch designed two churches in 'florid Gothic' (before Pugin had laid down strict canons for Gothic Revival), St. Mary Bathwick (1814–20) and St. Saviour, Larkhall (completed by his son 1829–32), while his son and successor was more at home with the Greek revival style now beginning to gain in influence. John Pinch senior, then, spans the end of the old and the beginning of the new.

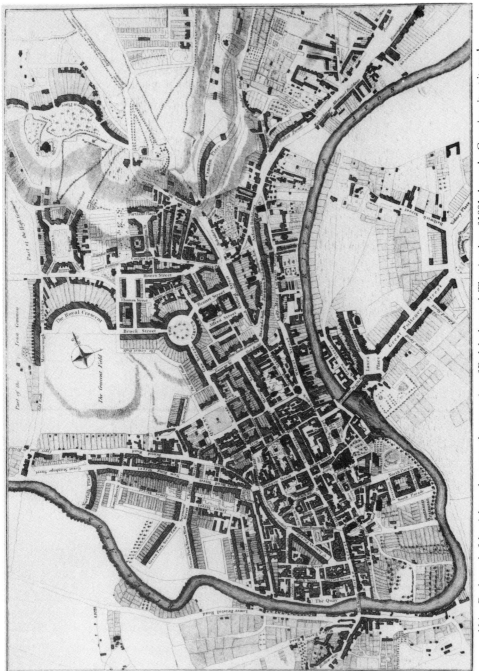

114. By the end of the eighteenth century the expansion of Bath had ceased. The city plan of 1801 shows the Georgian city at its peak. Terraces had spread up Lansdown and along the London Road but the Bathwick estate lay fossilized in its incompleteness.

But Bath was now essentially complete and even though the city's prosperity rallied after the Napoleonic Wars there was little expansion: what building there was was largely infill. New styles, therefore, tended to be swamped by the acres of Palladian. Greek revival made a brief appearance (ill. 115). The Lower Assembly Rooms were enlivened by a monumental Doric portico in 1807, built by William Wilkins, and after the building was destroyed by fire the portico was retained to aggrandize the new Scientific and Literary Institute put up in its stead. Wilkins, a foremost exponent of neo-classical architecture and designer of the National Gallery, was also responsible for the Ionic Masonic Hall (now Friends Meeting House) in York Street built in 1817, a fine but lonely example of the style. In the Upper Town, an even more memorable building, of quite uncompromising Greek revival mood, is the justly famous Doric House on Sion Hill built by J.M. Gandy about 1805 for the painter Thomas Baker. Other notable designs are Cleveland Place and Bridge created by H.E. Goodridge in 1827, as a second approach to the Bathwick estate, and the same architect's High Street frontage to The Corridor (1825). That there are so few neo-classical buildings worthy of consideration is a reflection of Bath's relative stagnation in the early decades of the nineteenth century.

Even the Gothic style so beloved of the Victorians and their immediate predecessors is very sparsely represented except for churches. Church building was prolific, particularly in the 1830s when new buildings were being erected at the rate of about one a year mostly in Gothic Revival style. A fine example if G.P. Manner's complete reconstruction of St. Michael, Broad Street

115. The early nineteenth century brought a new building style to Bath – Greek revival. That it was not extensively used in the city is a reflection of Bath's stagnation at the time. The example chosen here are the toll houses on Cleveland Bridge (H.E. Goodridge, 1827).

116. The medieval church of St. Michael, Broad Street was pulled down in 1742 and replaced by a classical building erected by the local stonemason John Harvey. In 1835 it was demolished and replaced by a delicate if slightly eccentric Gothic structure designed by the City Architect G.P. Manners. The tower is on the south side of the building forming a focus for the cross roads. Many of Bath's churches were built, or rebuilt in Gothic Revival style.

(1835–7) (ill. 116). The same architect was also responsible for a thoroughgoing restoration of the abbey where, among other improvements, he added pinnacles to the flying buttresses and turrets, evidently believing that this had been the intention of the original builders. Altogether Bath's ecclesiastical Gothic is comparatively innocuous and really rather dull.

Whilst the last of Bath's great terraces were being completed and the rash of suburban churches were spreading across the face of the city in preparation for the advent of the Victorian Sunday, attempts were being made to maintain something of the grand style of the past. Nowhere is this more impressively demonstrated than in the building of the Theatre Royal, on the south side of Beaufort Square, in a monumental style totally out of harmony with the gentle restraint of Strahan's early eighteenth century terraces. The theatre had previously been housed in Orchard Street but the old building was judged too small. Its grandiose replacement was designed by the London architect George Dance the younger and was erected by John Palmer in 1804–5. The sheer size of the building and the elaboration of its internal decoration leave little doubt that the Theatre Royal was intended to rival its London contemporaries, but seen in the context of Bath it represents the last defiant gesture of an age quickly passing. In 1872, after 50 years of unsteady fortune, the building was gutted by fire. Such was the mood of the time that serious doubts were expressed about the desirability of rebuilding. Bath was now in the throes of a depression, a change in dining habits made theatre-going inconvenient and, more important, Victorian mores had turned against such trivial and dangerous indulgences. Even so, within eleven months funds had been raised, the building completely renovated and the doors opened once more to allow Bathonians to enjoy the first night performance of Ellen Terry.

Nor were the bathing facilities overlooked. The King's Bath complex had been updated and enlarged at the end of the eighteenth century but the Hot Bath was much as Wood had left it. Now, in 1829, it was decided to extend the facilities by adding a large tepid bath reached through individual dressing rooms, each of which was fitted out with a fireplace for the added comfort of bathers. The plans were drawn up for the council by Decimus Burton and the work carried out by G.P. Manners in 1830. The new Tepid Bath together with Wood's Hot Bath created an establishment to rival the King's Bath facilities.

The employment of Burton, a well-known London architect, is in keeping with the mood of the times. In the eighteenth century, as we have seen, virtually every building was designed by a local man: in the first four decades of the nineteenth century the more important commissions went to outsiders – another example of the city's growing crisis of confidence.

Bath had been well-provided with pleasure gardens in the eighteenth century. Before the Bathwick estate was laid out the low-lying meadow on the east bank of the Avon had been the site of the popular Spring Gardens which could be reached only by boat, adding greatly to its enchantment. Later with the coming of Pulteney Bridge and the beginnings of the urban expansion east of the river, Sydney Gardens were created, while at about the same time Grosvenor Gardens were laid out, well out of the centre of town along the London road: both were private developments. In 1830, however, the Corporation took a hand and created the Royal Victoria Park on what was left of Barton fields. It at once became popular and fashionable but instead of providing recreation for a city as a whole it became the preserve of the middle classes through the simple expedient of wardens charged with removing anyone judged to be unclean or undesirable. The poor, whose need for open space and fresh air, away from their cramped, damp slums in Dolmeads, Avon Street and Holloway, was great, were thus effectively excluded.

The slums of Bath were notorious. Situated on the low-lying flood plain of the river, damp, ill-drained and unhygenic, the homes of the poor were ridden with disease and misery. Avon Street was worst of all (ill. 117). It had been built as middle class accommodation in 1730 but it soon became a through route for horses being led to water at the Avon and for materials of

117. Avon Street was built in the early eighteenth century to provide access from the newly constructed Avon wharfs to Kingsmead Square and the City. It soon became one of the city's notorious slums – a home for prostitution and disease. The street scene, photographed in 1890, gives some idea of the busy overcrowded atmosphere.

various sorts being carted to and from the city's wharf. This constant traffic combined with the ill-drained nature of the environment led to progressive decline until by the 1830s the whole area had become an appalling slum. When an epidemic of cholera hit the city in 1831 more than half those who died came from Avon Street. Ten years later the Revd. Elwin in his contribution to the report of the Sanitary Commissioners 1842, could write: 'I went through the registers from the commencement and observed that, whatever contagious or epidemic disease prevailed, – fever, smallpox, influenza, (Avon Street) was the scene of its principal ravages; and it is the very place of which every person acquainted with Bath would have predicted the result. Everything vile and offensive is congregated there. All the scum of Bath – its low prostitutes, its thieves, its beggars – are piled up in the dens rather than the houses of which the street consists'. When it is remembered that one in twenty-five of the population of Bath at this time lived in the slums of the Avon Street district then the nature of the city begins to take on a new perspective. Across the river, Holloway was little better: it was the haunt of the itinerant beggars who came to prey on Bath. John Earle describes it vividly in 1874, 'In proportion as the Squares and Crescents filled with the affluent, the dens of Holloway filled with beggars. This was their camp from whence they watched the visitors who were their prey, and eluded the Corporation who were their natural enemies .... Bath, which enjoyed a pre-eminence in other things, was equally distinguished for its colony of beggars. Holloway was a parody of Bath. As the fine shops of Bath got in their new and fashionable goods at the approach of the Season, so the petty chandlers of Holloway . . . were constantly forced to double their orders at the same epoch. As the price of lodgings varied in Bath according to an understood attraction so in Holloway was there a like variety offered to the selection of the professional beggar'.

So Regency Bath for all its pretence of calm elegance was little different from any other city of the industrial revolution. Class differences were rampant and the poor suffered. There is no more telling statistic than the average age of death at Bath recorded in 1841:

Gentlemen and Professional persons	55
Tradesmen and farmers	37
Mechanics and labourers	25

Appalling though these figures are from a present-day

viewpoint, Bath was a surprisingly healthy place compared with much of the rest of England: at Liverpool a gentleman might expect to die at 35, a labourer at 15.

In spite of the poverty Bath was a comparatively stable place throughout the difficult years of reform. The lower classes were deprived and disease-ridden by our standards, but the well-being of the city was not dependent on fickle industry dragging the fortunes of the workers into periodic troughs of despair: it was buffered against rapid economic change by its massive resident middle class population. G.S. Gibbes, in *The Bath Visitant* (1839) sums up the very fabric of the community: '. . . Bath is not a city of trade. No manufacturer worthy of notice is carried on within its limits, nor is it the resort of commerce. . . . Bath is best fitted for the retirement of individuals with independent incomes, whether small or large. For those past the meridian of life, its quietness, beautiful neighbourhood, and warmth of climate, particularly recommend it. . . . Trade in Bath consists principally in the sale of articles connected with the refinements, rather than the necessities of life'.

118. The Kennet and Avon Canal reached Bath between 1796 and 1810 ending in three large canal basins in Dolemeads at the point where the canal joins the Avon. The canal crossed the Bathwick estate and where it passed through Sydney Gardens good use was made of it as a landscape feature. Most of its bridges were designed by John Rennie and cast in Coalbrookdale. J.C. Nattes' aquatint was published in 1805.

In the four city parishes of St. James, St. Peter and St. Paul, St. Michael's and Walcot the total working population was 17,713, of whom a third were employed in some form of domestic service as housekeepers, charwomen, cooks, gardeners, etc. Eleven per cent worked in clothing manufacture while another 11 per cent were small craftsmen such as cabinet-makers, locksmiths, wheel-chair makers and the like; 9 per cent were shop keepers, 7.7 per cent were builders, 5.9 per cent were professional men such as surgeons, solicitors, 4 per cent offered entertainment or hospitality, while 3.9 per cent provided more menial service. In other words nearly 90 per cent of the working population living in the central parishes were involved wholly or substantially in providing goods and services for the wealthy consumers living, usually in retirement, in the more salubrious areas of the Upper Town and Bathwick. The city produced for its own consumption and all the time that its large resident population 'past the meridian of life' could afford to maintain its standards of living the working classes were provided with a level of stability unknown in the industrial cities of early Victorian England.

The early decades of the nineteenth century saw Bath firmly linked to the communications network that was fast engulfing Britain. First to come was the Kennet and Avon Canal planned in 1797 but not completed until 1810. It was a major achievement allowing goods to be transported from London to Bristol in just 4 days. On the last stage of its journey the canal wound its way across the low-lying plain to the east of the city ending in three basins at Dolmeads just opposite the Hams before joining the uncanalized river. En route it traversed Sydney Gardens passing through the 'delightful groves, pleasant vistas and charming lawns' where the canal was put to good use as a landscape feature enlivened, we are told, 'with two elegant cast-iron bridges thrown over it, after the manner of the Chinese' (ill. 118).

The canal company had enjoyed barely 25 years of return on its colossal investment when the Great Western Railway Bills were put before parliament. The first was rejected but the second, to build a through line from London to Bristol, received the Royal Assent in 1835. It spelt doom for the canal and in spite of orchestrated opposition the line was finally opened for its entire length in 1841 (ills. 119 and 120).

Many saw in the coming of the railway the salvation of Bath's flagging popularity. Certainly for the working classes it provided a limited blessing. In the boom years of 1839–41 when the major constructional work was underway labour was at a

119 and 120.   Isambard Kingdom Brunel's broad gauge railway from London to Bristol opened in 1841. It changed the face of the city adding its own majestic architecture. The station itself was once roofed, shown in this contemporary water-colour of 1846 (ill. 119). Where the line cut through Sydney Gardens the cutting was carefully landscaped (the water-colour of the cutting, ill. 120, is also of 1846). In Bath the railway in all its aspects made a positive addition to the townscape.

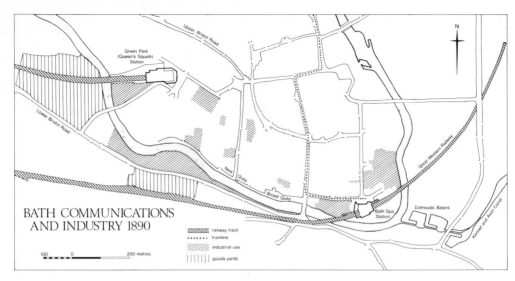

121.   In the nineteenth century the south part of Bath became the centre of the communications network. The medieval city bridge was the beginning. Then, in the early eighteenth century the quays along the north bank of the Avon were extended and improved. The Kennet and Avon Canal opened in 1810 bringing the canal basins to Dolemeads at the point where the canal joined the Avon. Brunel's Great Western Railway arrived in 1840–1 his station and its immediate approach enabling him to complete the southern end of Wood's Grand Forum scheme (compare ill. 93). Finally in 1869–70 the Midland Railway terminus was built. Queens Square Station (Green Park Station) served as the link north to Birmingham and south to the south coast. (Source: author).

122.   The Great Western Railway viaduct, designed to carry the line across the river and the approach road to the southern side of the city, is much like the entrance to a Cambridge college.

premium and labourers' wages soared by 25 per cent, but it was a short-term benefit and when the expected economic miracle failed to materialize, Bath settled down to a quarter of a century of genteel decline.

Brunel's railway changed the face of southern Bath (ill. 121). Sweeping across Bathwick and through Dolmeads it just touched the southern edge of the Hams and crossed the river again on the spectacular Skew Bridge and viaduct, taking it above the road junction opposite the old bridge, before slicing through another wedge of working class housing en route to Bristol. The station and Skew Bridge viaduct are both notable pieces of architecture. The viaduct is typical of Brunel. Its battlemented style, complete with turrets and heavily moulded late 'Gothic' doorways is strongly reminiscent of the frontage of a Cambridge college. It has no place in Bath but yet does not seem at all inappropriate to its alien function. The station, on the other hand, in restrained Jacobeathan, with its obligatory mullioned windows, blends far more harmoniously with its setting because it is faced in Bath stone. Both station and approach were carefully planned. Two new roads were laid out: Dorchester Street led westwards to join Southgate Street near the city bridge, while Manvers Street led northwards to become one with John Wood's Pierrepoint Street. This was intended to be the grand approach to Bath. The two corners facing the station were both graced with fine buildings in Bath Georgian – the Royal Hotel and the Manvers Arms (later the Argyll Hotel). Both were designed as the corner members of terraces lining the two new streets, but in the economic climate of the time the challenge was not taken up by the local builders, and only later was the area developed in an ad hoc and visually disastrous manner. The least that can be said is that Brunel made a carefully considered attempt to integrate his railway with the architecture of the city. That the approach is now a dismal failure is no fault of his.

While the coming of the railway did little to lift the sagging fortunes of the city, it helped to crystallize Bath's industrial zone in the southern part of the city along the Lower Bristol Road towards Twerton where the mills and the foundaries tended to congregate. It was here that the transport networks – the main road, the river with its quays and the railway goods yard converged, and inevitably it was here amid the noise and dirt that the working class lived (ill. 121).

Nearly thirty years after Brunel's line came into being, Bath's second station was built, nosing incongruously into the western fringe of the Green Park development. Queen's Square Station,

as it was known for most of its life (but more recently Green Park Station), was built in 1869–70 as the terminus of a spur of the Bristol–Birmingham line. A few years later (1874) the station was linked to the Somerset and Dorset line. The building of the Midland Railway terminal should not be seen as part of the same process that brought the Great Western. The two events are separated by three decades during which the fortunes of Bath were at a low ebb – rather it is the beginning of a new era for in the 1860s the City Fathers began at last to take a more aggressive and dynamic attitude to Bath's needs. Innovations were afoot which, if successful, would re-establish Bath as one of the country's premier spas.

The crisis came to a head in 1864. By this time the post of Master of Ceremonies, so effectively held a century and a half before by Beau Nash, had been made redundant, and the Corporation had even attempted to let the baths on lease, but after a trial period the lessee had terminated the agreement and

123. Green Park Station was built in 1869–70 at a time when Bath's prosperity was beginning to pick up. Originally it was designed as the terminal for the Midland Railway from Birmingham but in 1874 the station was linked to the Somerset and Dorset Railway. The building, for long derelict, now finds a new lease of life as a shopping precinct.

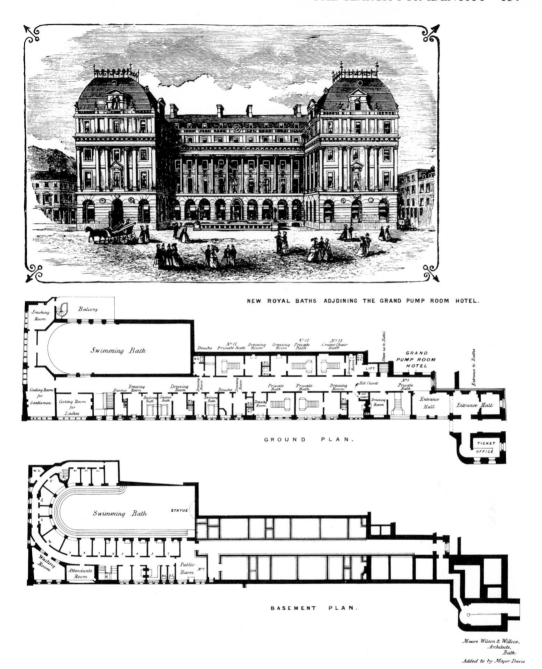

NEW ROYAL BATHS ADJOINING THE GRAND PUMP ROOM HOTEL.

124 and 125.   In an attempt to revitalize the spa the City Fathers decided to build a vast modern hotel in Stall Street opposite the Pump Room to replace the derelict White Hart Hotel. The Grand Pump Room Hotel was opened in 1869. One of the attractions of the new hotel was the proximity of a suite of baths – the New Royal Baths – reached by lifts from the hotel and providing every facility for the elderly and the infirm. The hotel was demolished in 1959; the baths are now derelict and about to be destroyed.

nobody else could be found to take it on. One by one the
city's hotels closed: York House was turned into a post office
and in 1864 the famous White Hart, immediately opposite the
Pump Room, shut its doors for ever. It was in this atmosphere of
deepening gloom that the mayor addressed the Corporation.
'Having thought much lately of the change that Bath has
undergone I, have come to the conclusion that we ought to make
a vigorous effort to revive its prosperity and that we cannot do
better than follow the old lines'. It was hardly a novel idea, but it
caught the mood of the time and a committee was duly set up.
What they proposed was to create a grand new hotel to replace
the White Hart, complete with lifts to take patients to a
basement level where the most up-to-date bathing facilities
awaited them.

After various financial problems the Grand Pump Room
Hotel was opened in 1869 (ill. 124). The bath, built with
Corporation money, opened two years earlier. 'Everyone who
sees the beautiful suite of baths adjoining the hotel . . . sees also
what the city has gained in this respect. Conveyed by a lift from
bedroom floors, the patient is not subject to hazardous and
comfortless exposure, while the variety of baths, suited to
various forms of complaint, is a great advantage . . . at the end of
a spacious corridor, was added a swimming bath of magnificent
proportions surrounded by dressing-rooms; the architecture of
the entire building being worthy of the ancient city'. Seventy
years after this monument to civic expectation was opened it was
taken over for offices by the Navy during the Second World
War. It never reopened and was eventually demolished in 1959.
The baths 'worthy of the ancient city' lasted longer but now lie
derelict awaiting destruction. Nonetheless, after an unsteady
start, the Grand Pump Room Hotel began to attract an
increasing number of visitors and a gradual, but distinct, revival
got underway: 'all the best hotels have profited by the improved
state of things; another of much repute has been opened in a
good situation; private family hotels have multiplied, houses and
lodgings have been better let'.

Throughout the next two decades medical science advanced
but Bath was determined not to be left behind. Dr. Henry
Freeman, surgeon to the Royal United Hospital and later
mayor, and Major Charles Davis, City Surveyor, were sent on
an extended tour of foreign spas to study the new treatments
that were now in vogue. Their report encouraged the city to
embark upon a complete new suite of baths – the Douche and
Massage Baths – which were built on the York-Stall Street
corner and opened in 1889. The building itself, diminutive in

Hot Mineral Springs
OF BATH.

Douche, Massage, Thermal-Vapour,
&c.

DAILY YIELD OF SPRINGS, 507,600 GALLONS AT 120° F.

OUNDED by the Romans in the First
Century.
ΑΡΙΣΤΟΝ ΜΕΝ ΥΔΩΡ.
BATHERS DURING 1888,
94,835.

These Baths are unrivalled in Europe for luxury
and extent, and contain all that modern improvements can
provide for the comfort and relief of the invalid, or the
enjoyment of those in health.

EXPERIENCED DOUCHEURS AND DOUCHEUSES
Are employed to carry out efficiently the system of

Douche, Inhalation, Aspiration, Pulverisation,
Thermal-Vapour, &c.,
ADOPTED AT CONTINENTAL SPAS.

The Medical Profession send Patients who suffer from Gout,
Rheumatism, Sciatica, Neuralgia, Paralysis, Disorders of the
Digestive System, Metallic Poisoning, Eczema, Psoriasis, and all
the Scaly Diseases of the Skin.

Letters to the General Manager will receive every attention.

126 and 127. The
Douche and Massage
Baths, opened in 1889,
provided the visitor with
a new range of facilities
as the contemporary
advertisement proclaims
(ill. 127). The
photograph (ill. 126),
taken about 1914, shows
a surprisingly composed
patient undergoing the
Four-Cell or Schnee
Bath treatment against a
background of Major
Davis' High Victorian
decor. The Baths were
demolished in 1972.

scale and fussy in detail, contained a complete suite of the new 'Continental' treatment – the Aix-les- Bains douche, the Berthold Vapour Bath, an Inhalation-room, a Pulverization-room and so on. 'These rooms are lighted high up under arched ceilings, and are tiled round, having handsome Roman Tesserae as flooring' (ill. 126). The new treatment was an instant success and visitor revenue doubled almost overnight. Everything from stiff neck and muscular rheumatism to Scrivener's palsy and Hysterical Paralysis could be treated by Savoyards trained and experienced at Aix – 'Their rapidity, delicate touch, and general manipulation in *Massage* indicate a natural adaptation to their functions, in which it is said they take some kind of hereditary pride' – the shades of new-fangled Darwinism were even reaching Bath! But fashions in medicine are short-lived and the baths, long derelict by 1972, were demolished to make way for an office block.

It is an amusing coincidence that the attempts to revive the spa between 1867 and 1889 brought to light one of Bath's greatest assets which had previously passed largely unnoticed – its Roman past.

When the Pump Room was built in 1790 part of the loose blocks forming the pediment of the Temple of Sulis Minerva came to light, causing a flurry of excitement, but little was done to follow up the find and there matters rested until 1864 when the old White Hart Hotel closed. It was at this time that Sir Gilbert Scott was restoring the abbey and in his employ, as Clerk of Works, was a keen and able antiquarian, James Irvine. Irvine, knowing of the discoveries of 1790, reasoned that the body of the temple probably lay beneath the hotel, and as soon as it closed he undertook exploratory excavations. When demolition and rebuilding got underway between 1867–9 he was constantly on site recording with meticulous accuracy everything of interest exposed. The results were not spectacular and it is only in the light of recent work that their importance has been realized.

For much of the next decade Irvine was enthusing the City Surveyor, Major Davis, with the discoveries he was making in and around the abbey. In this way Davis was introduced to the great Roman outfall drain which led him to discover and excavate the Roman reservoir built around the original spring-head beneath the King's Bath. This was completed in 1878–9 and the next year we find Davis beginning to uncover the Great Bath amid much excitement (ills. 128 and 129).

It is greatly to the credit of the city authorities that they immediately saw the potential of the Roman site. An Antiquities

128 and 129.   The 1880s saw the excavation of the Roman Baths in the centre of the city. Ill. 128 shows the excavations in progress beneath the partially destroyed Queens Bath. Ill. 129 is a view of the Great Bath at about this time showing the Roman structures largely uncared for and suffering from the weather while decisions were being made how best to cover and protect them.

Committee was set up and funds were raised to clear the Great Bath. But from the outset there were problems: local tradesmen took the council to court for causing a nuisance, extra money had to be raised to buy the Poor Law Offices which jutted out over the Roman establishment, but worse still Major Davis, evidently a quarrelsome man, entered into a vitriolic public debate about who had first discovered the baths. The situation became even more heated a few years later when, in 1886, Davis began work on the new Douche and Massage Baths which were to be built above the west end of the Roman bathing establishment. He was in an unenviable position: as a servant of the council he was charged with erecting the new baths with the minimum of delay and cost, but as an antiquarian he was under pressure to preserve the archaeological remains beneath. A further torrent of abuse showered down on the poor man and a commission of enquiry was set up which guardedly exonerated him. When, in 1972, the Douche and Massage Baths were pulled down, it became possible to appreciate the enormous care which Davis had taken over the Roman features: his solutions to difficult structural problems were immaculate and he emerges as a man of skill and integrity.

When the new baths opened in 1889 it was possible for visitors to view the Roman remains. The Circular Bath had been covered but the Great Bath was still open to the sky and had suffered nearly nine years of erosion through exposure. Some thing of the muddled and unsatisfactory nature of the exhibit can be judged from contemporary photographs (ill. 128). It was clear that more work had to be undertaken to integrate the Roman remains with the Pump Room complex and with this in mind, in 1892, the Pump Room extension scheme was first mooted. The intention was to cover and make more presentable the Roman baths while at the same time creating a new concert room to relieve the overcrowding of the existing Pump Room. A brief was agreed and the project was put out to competition. The events which ensued read like a Victorian farce. Major Davis, who but for a minor error, should have been appointed architect, was kept out of the competition by his enemies who managed to change the brief at the last moment. The full story is a fascinating insight into the devious working of Victorian local government and of the personality clashes which Bath was suffering. Natural justice was not done and Davis was the victim.

The result of all this is the situation we inherit today. Instead of the Roman Bath being covered by a vaulted roof as it had been in the Roman period (and as Davis well knew and wanted to reproduce) it is now open and surrounded only by a visually confusing colonnade of totally inappropriate a scale. This was entirely the result of the council rewriting the brief ostensibly to cut costs but in reality to exclude Davis. The London architect J.M. Brydon won the competition and his is the grand Concert Room that stands next to the Pump Room.

The Roman Bath and Pump Room extension was completed in 1897. Brydon's exterior is remarkably successful, given the difficult nature of the match he had to effect. He chose to build what was visually a separate building, more massive and baroque than Baldwin's original but nonetheless attractive in its own right and perfectly in keeping with its context. The concert hall interior is magnificent: the only sadness is that acoustically it is the worst hall in Bath.

Brydon was a good choice and a safe bet. He had already been employed in Bath, from 1891, to enlarge Baldwin's Guildhall.

130. The last monument to Victorian Bath (a monument it most certainly is) is the Empire Hotel, a mountain of eclectic styles designed by Major Davis and completed in 1901. Davis had been thwarted many times and grandiose schemes he had put forward came to nothing – the Empire Hotel project gave him his chance (and some would say, his revenge). To his credit, he was the first (and only) architect to recognize the immense value of the riverside – his hotel exploited this. The road he built in front of it, joining Orange Grove to Pulteney Bridge, still provides one of the most memorable vistas to be had of the rural setting of the city.

131. The other face of Victorian Bath: life at the Pig and Whistle, Avon Street through the eyes of Robert Cruikshank

This he did with considerable skill adding two wings set back from Baldwin's main front, and with lower roof lines, but otherwise matching the style of the original quite closely. He had shown himself to be an architect of originality but one with a deep-rooted respect for his predecessors. Brydon's two buildings symbolized Bath's growing pride in itself: after a long period of uncertainty it seemed at last that the city was about to take off on a new flight of prosperity.

As if to force home and point, in 1899 work began on a new purpose-built hotel – the Empire Hotel (ill. 130). Occupying a prime site in the city overlooking the Avon, Pulteney Bridge and the abbey, this seven-storeyed monolithic monster dominates the lower city. It is a remarkable, eclectic piece of nonsense, five sober storeys topped by a fanciful facade of incongruous gables and towers. No-one loves it. It is written off as an arrogant indulgence – a typical 'overwhelming' and 'disastrous' *fin de siecle* erection, too gross for Bath and totally lacking in quality. And yet there is something in it that catches the imagination: it has a bombastic energy typical of its time. Although by any standards the Empire Hotel lacks harmony and elegance, Bath would be the poorer without it.

We have omitted to mention the architect – it was Major Davis. A forceful and difficult man, Davis was the centre of controversy for 20 years. He uncovered the Roman baths and ensured their preservation, engendering totally unwarranted abuse throughout the 1880s, and in the 1890s he was cheated of his chance to complete the project with a cover building. But in 1899 his great moment arrived with the commission to design the Empire Hotel. Is it too fanciful to suppose that in this great elephantine structure Davis was getting his own back? – at the very least it is a monument to an unlovable but nonetheless notable local personality.

The Empire Hotel and the parade, which was created in front of it, mark the end of an era. Bath's late Victorian prosperity was over. While the population grew steadily throughout the first four decades of the twentieth century the life and energy of the city had sapped away. The mood of the place is captured perfectly in a guidebook description of the 1920s: 'Bath has its value as a health resort, particularly to invalids in the winter time; for the air is peculiarly sweet and fresh, and the encircling hills protect the city from cold winds. . . . It is justly claimed that scarcely any other English town is graced with suburbs so bracing as these air-swept heights. In a recent year 1921 the death-rate was at the remarkably low figure of 10.3 per 1000'.

8. TOWARDS A FUTURE

THE GRIME-ENCRUSTED BATH of the 1930s was a drab place of little charm. Many of its fine eighteenth-century buildings had been Victorianized: the Pump Room and Assembly Rooms interiors were grossly overdecorated and dowdy, plate glass shop fronts in ornate surrounds defaced the grandeur of Milsom Street, while the terraces and cresents were taking on a variegated, ad hoc, appearance as windows were lowered and given sashes, chimney stacks mutated into a variety of shapes and sizes, and rotting balustrades and cornices were variously patched. Yet amid it all there were some sparks of hope. In 1931 the Assembly Rooms had been purchased and given to the National Trust so that 'this fine building will again play a dignified and harmonious part in the life and letters of this beautiful city' (Lord Crawford). Work began restoring it to its former glory almost immediately and in 1938 the refurbished structure emerged, crisp, clean and shorn of all its irrelevant accretions. This was the beginning of a new awareness.

A year later, however, the scene in Bath changed dramatically when, at the outbreak of war, more than half of the Admiralty staff was moved to the city from London. Hotels, museums and schools were requisitioned within the centre and overspill estates of hutments were built in the hills and valleys around. The grime of the city was now matched by the grim atmosphere of the early war years.

On the nights of 25 and 26 April, 1942 Bath suffered two devastating bombing raids mounted by the bombers of Luftflotte III as a reprisal for the RAF bombing of Lübeck and Rostock. Four hundred and seventeen people were killed, over 1000 buildings were destroyed or damaged beyond repair and another 2000 suffered damage of some kind. The 'Baedeker raids', as they were called, were designed by the German High Command to destroy cultural targets in selected British cities, but in Bath they largely failed to achieve that end. Though some parts of the Georgian city suffered, the damage was comparatively slight: the Assembly Rooms were gutted, part of the south side of Queen's Square was destroyed and holes were smashed in the Paragon. Bombs in the Circus and the Royal Crescent burnt out individual buildings and some areas along Julian Road were flattened, but given the potential for large-scale devastation the escape of so much of Georgian Bath was remarkable. It was the west and south of the city that bore the brunt of the attack. Around the GWR station the bombs fell thick, St. James' Church near South gate and Abbey Church House and Westgate Buildings were gutted and large areas of

Kingsmead, Holloway, Oldfield Park and Green Park were severely damaged (ill. 132). It was in these western suburbs with their high density residential development that loss of life was greatest. The rubble was cleared, dangerous structures demolished but the gaps remained.

As the war drew to a close a Joint Planning Committee, under Sir Patrick Abercromby, was set up to prepare a plan for rebuilding, and in February 1945 the *Plan for Bath* was presented to the public. It was a bold attempt to provide a framework in which the city could rebuild and expand. In many ways it was a far-sighted scheme: it expressed the need for neighbourhood housing, sited on the edges of the built-up area but below Bath's belt of green hill-crests so as to retain the city's close visual link with the countryside: it set out to maintain the network of medieval streets in the city core, largely unaltered, by siphoning off the through traffic: and it stated for the first time that the Avon was a much under-used asset. There were also less attractive elements: the proposed ring road following the line of the walls would have been an environmental disaster, constricting the heart of the city within a torniquet of traffic; the proposed large-scale clearances of what was left of

132.   Large areas of Bath were devasted in the 'Baedeker raids' of April 1942. The suburbs suffered the most. One area to receive a direct hit was the King Edward Road, Oldfield Park: the blast damage was extensive.

Kingsmead, including the demolition of the baroque Rosewell House, would have been an unpardonable error of judgment; while the evident approval of Georgian pastiche as a building style was a feeble response to the very real problems of rebuilding Bath. Nonetheless the plan was a valuable exercise, and even though little of it has been realized, it had the effect of focusing people's attention on Bath, as a developing organic whole, in a way that had never before been attempted.

Rebuilding got slowly underway. The damage in the Paragon, the Circus, the Cresent and Queen's Square was quickly made good and where necessary facades were replaced in precise replica. Abbey Church House was substantially rebuilt in 1952 and in 1963 the re-restored Assembly Rooms were once more opened to the public.

But after the decade of gentle infill and careful patching Bath was plunged into a nightmare which was to last unabated for almost twenty years. It was a time of wholesale destruction of the most mindless kind to make way for a variety of redevelopment schemes almost invariably of a scale and quality totally unsympathetic to Bath. Hundreds and hundreds of eighteenth and early nineteenth century buildings, mainly artisan dwellings, were bulldozed flat irrespective of the fact that many of them were listed as buildings of note under the Town and Country Planning Act of 1947 (ill. 133). What many people today would

133. 'Improvement schemes' of the 1960s were responsible for devastating vast areas of Bath's eighteenth and nineteenth century suburbs. Philip Street is seen here in the course of obliteration.

regard as successive acts of vandalism were proposed, debated and approved by the Local Planning authority with the support of the elected representatives. No laws were broken, no corners cut – it was the democratic process at work deliberately modifying Bath in a way which seemed to those in power to be in the best interests of the community. When the City Architect said, 'If you want to keep Georgian artisans' houses, then you will have to find Georgian artisans to live in them' we can only suppose that he genuinely believed that restoration and renovation were not viable alternatives to demolition and rebuilding.

And yet throughout this period local and national amenity groups were pleading for a halt, pointing out the inestimable value of what was being destroyed. Some notable battles were won: Beaufort Square (*c.* 1730), Kingsmead Square (1730s), New Bond Street (1806–1810) were all saved from annihilation or mutilation. But these few bright spots must be seen against the black tide of demolition which swept through the city.

The destruction of so much of the eighteenth and nineteenth century city was bad enough, but when the new buildings put up as replacements are considered, the full magnitude of the disaster becomes apparent. Very little good can be said of any of them and virtually all have come in for strong criticism or outright abuse from a variety of writers whose opinions deserve respect. Adam Fergusson in his frightening book *The Sack of Bath*, which vividly portrays the city's nightmare period, describes the residential development in Ballance Street as 'grotesque products of bureaucratic minds fuddled by an architectural challenge they have never understood'. Many would find his judgment too mild. It is not just that the new buildings are largely lacking in quality (another over-generous judgment) but the majority of them are totally out of scale for their contexts. The vulgar mass-produced monotony of the Marks and Spencers and Woolworths building (ill. 135) might be innocuous in many a suburban High Street but in the medieval core of Bath it is an insult, even more so because in construction it has destroyed a considerable length of the city wall, the ancient Ham Gate, a length of St. James Street (a late Saxon and medieval street line) and the medieval church of St. James. How this could have been allowed to happen in 1959 is beyond comprehension.

Everyone who has made the depressing tour of Bath's modern architecture will have their pet-hates and there will be as many views as there are viewers, but all agree that something went dreadfully wrong. For two decades the judgment and the sensibilities of those in power – the planners, the elected

committee members and the eminent advisors hired by the city – were seriously at fault. In a carefully balanced foreword to Adam Fergusson's book, Lord Goodman wrote, 'It is unhappily the case that most of the scenic and architectural desecrations that happen arise, not from malice, but from folly – since stupidity is even more difficult to control than evil'. Perhaps even this is too harsh a judgment: could it not simply have been that the problem was too great for the capabilities of those who had to face it?

134 and 135. Many modern buildings, while paying lip service to Georgian proportions were assembled in monotonous baulk heedless of their environmental impact. Witness the lifeless Woolworths/Marks and Spencers emporium (ill. 135) totally out of keeping with the city's historic core which its construction helped destroy. The Beaufort Hotel (*above*) leaves one speechless.

The issues are too fresh and the wounds too raw for the nightmare years to be seen in perspective. But let us remember that hideously out of proportion though the Empire Hotel was (and still is) its very size and eccentricity are beginning to give it a certain period charm. Perhaps, eighty years on, the same will be said of one or two of the 1955–75 vintage. At a guess the only structure of the clutch worth backing is Sir Frederick Gibberd's Bath Technical College – but we must wait and see.

Another of the running battles of the 1960s was traffic. Fortunately it was a battle fought more on paper than in the streets. Bath had for some time been experiencing a build-up in traffic, much of it through traffic, and the city decided to commission Colin Buchanan and Partners to produce a report which was duly presented in 1965. The essential recommendations were to divert the A4 to a new line across Bathwick Meadows and to lead it in a tunnel beneath the Upper Town emerging by the bowling green on the Upper Bristol Road to become meshed in a massive interchange scheme. Another new road, partly in cutting and partly tunnel, was to take local traffic from a Walcot Street interchange on an east-west axis just south of Queen's Square. The scheme squarely faced the prospect of increasing traffic and proposed a solution based on careful research and a full appreciation of Bath's very special needs. However, it came at a time when the fight to save Bath was at its height and people were coming more and more to reject change simply because it was change. What they had seen in the guise of 'planning' and 'improvement' was disastrous: all plans, therefore, were immediately suspect. The arguments were long and vitriolic and, after the initial furore, the debate became protracted. Now, twenty years on, the existing road network, carefully rethought, seems to be coping quite adequately.

The mood in the country as a whole was now beginning to change. It was at last being recognized that road schemes and redevelopment appropriate for cities like Birmingham were not suited to ancient towns like Bath. In 1966 four historic towns, Bath, Chester, Chichester and York, were chosen to serve as case studies in order to 'discover how to reconcile our old towns with in the twentieth century without actually knocking them down' (Anthony Greenwood, Minister of Housing and Local Government). 'They are a great cultural asset, and, with the growth of tourism they are increasingly an economic asset as well'. To carry out the Bath study Buchanan and Partners were appointed and their report *Bath: a study in conservation* was published in 1968. What effectively it did was to show how, with attention to detail and using imagination, the core of Bath could

be made to live and to earn its living while maintaining its integrity as an historic centre. It is ironic that as the report was being prepared considerable areas of eighteenth century building outside the historic core were being flattened.

Local government reorganization in 1974 brought with it many changes – changes in personnel and changes in attitudes. More important it provided a break point at which old ideas and allegiances could be cast off without loss of face and new causes could be espoused. It was perhaps no coincidence that immediately after the change-over the Secretary of State for the Environment wrote to the City Council saying that he would be prepared to finance substantially the preparation of a medium-term programme for the conservation of the city as part of a three-pronged approach, the two other studies being the effects of Minimum Physical Change and Traffic Management experiments. These studies were to be co-ordinated by a Steering Group set up by the Department of the Environment. Further negotiations led to the undertaking that the DOE would, in addition, fund a special programme of conservation in the city over a five year period. The area under consideration was 3360 acres of the city's Conservation Area.

The more sceptical observer would see this as a clear case of National Government taking the advantage of the trauma of reorganization to let it be known that it was far from satisfied with events in Bath, and to offer gentle guidance in the right direction. How much this was due to the clamour of opposition to the blunders of the previous administration, and how much to a growing awareness of conservation issues, it is impossible to say. What is important from the point of view of Bath is that the nightmare period of massive redevelopment ended, to be followed by a rational period of careful reconsideration undertaken by a team of highly skilled professionals brought up to understand that there is more to a city than the newly-built amenities it can boast. The report, significantly entitled *Saving Bath: a programme for conservation*, was published in 1978 and provides the strategy that is now being followed.

Standing back from it all Bath's post-war history can be divided into two cycles. The first, following the devastation of the Second World War, began with a plan (Abercromby 1945) and was followed by a period of slow change which developed a momentum during the period 1955–74. The second cycle grew out of a reaction to the unacceptable results of the first. It too began with plans (Buchanan 1968 and *Saving Bath* 1978). We are now in the phase of slow change. Whether or not there will be an escalation and with what results we must wait and see. But perhaps it is significant that the authors of *Saving Bath* have chosen to print on the title page a quotation from Macaulay, 'The smallest actual good is better than the most magnificent promises of impossibilities'.

Post-war Bath is in many ways a microcosm of Britain's planning dilemma. It demonstrates more sharply than anywhere the confrontation between two opposing philosophies: good planning means large-scale redevelopment / good planning means large-scale conservation. The first can be characterized by old terraces truncated by new roads and solitary out-of-proportion buildings set in geometrical areas of civic grass; the second by precious self-effacing infill, and concrete tubs sprouting vegetation carefully placed to break the monotony of interminable pedestrian precincts. Which is right? The success of a planning strategy can only be judged by the degree of long-term contentment felt by those who live within its constraints.

The Bath of the 1980s is a new Bath. The grime has gone, the pace has quickened and the average age has been reduced. It is fast finding a new identity as a place which is fun to be in. The Bath Festival creates a feeling of season while the buskers of Union Street cater for everyone. It is certainly a delightful town to visit (all those tourists cannot be wrong) but is it a congenial place to live in? Amid the perfection of the eighteenth-century architecture, the elegant shop-displays of expensive Italian furniture and the overpowering smell of herbal goodness wafting from innumerable boutiques, one can long for the sheer tacky vulgarity of the bus station or the comic brashness of Southgate Street. The fascination of a city lies in its variety and its contrasts. These exist in plenty in Bath: it will be a pity if timid introspection prevents our generation and the next from making their mistakes on a sufficient scale to amuse and to annoy our successors. A city is not just a medium for living: it must be a stimulant for life.

WHAT TO READ

IT IS VERY DIFFICULT for an academic, writing a book of this kind, not to qualify every statement with footnotes and references: to do so might give the book a more scholarly appearance (some even judge scholarship by the length of the footnotes!) but it would make it very tiresome to read. Yet to leave the text unsupported would be unfair to those readers who want to learn more. We have, therefore, adopted a compromise. In the section below (pp. 179) an extensive bibliography is provided, including all the published works specifically about Bath that have been consulted while writing this book. They are listed, according to the Harvard style of referencing, by author and date of publication in two separate lists: A dealing with books and pamphlets and B with shorter papers in journals and books. The notes offered here are intended to serve as a bridge between the main body of the book and the bibliography.

Before getting into too much detail, where should a reader who wishes to become gently immersed in the subject begin? Certainly with no more than six books – but which? An excellent introduction is Bryan Little's *The Building of Bath* (Little 1947) which spans the entire period of the city's development. This together with John Haddon's *Bath* (Haddon 1973) are essential reading. For the Roman period my own *Roman Bath Discovered* (Cunliffe 1971, second edition 1984) covers the ground while for Saxon and Medieval Bath chapters 3 and 4 above are the fullest general survey available. The eighteenth century is very well served. Edith Sitwell's *Bath* (Sitwell 1932) is an elegant introduction and will lead naturally to Walter Ison's *Georgian Buildings of Bath* (Isons 1948, reprinted 1969). The more recent period is treated with passion in Adam Fergusson's *The Sack of Bath* (Fergusson 1973). Finally, by far the best guide to the city is Charles Robertson's *Bath, an Architectural Guide* (Robertson 1975) which no visitor should be without.

Having dipped into these books the reader may then wish to get down to specific questions. Let me suggest then, chapter by chapter, where to begin. To save space I will quote only author and date which can be checked for detail of title and publisher in the two bibliographies.

Chapter 1   Landscape and Man

There are few general books and you will have to search specialist journals. The mystery of the springs is explained in convincing detail in Andrews et al. 1982 while in Kellaway 1985 you will find an up-to-date summary of the geomorphology of Bath. A fascinating account of the problem of dealing with the springs is given in Armstrong 1838.

The early prehistoric settlement around Bath is explored in Williams 1950, Grimes 1960 and Tratman 1973 while for the later prehistoric (Iron Age) sites mentioned read Cunliffe 1984a for a general introduction and for specific sites: Little Solsbury (Dowden 1957 and 1962); Bathampton (Wainwright 1967); and Budbury (Wainwright 1970). Two recent books deal thoroughly with the archaeology of the area: Gloucestershire (Saville (ed.) 1984) and Somerset (Aston & Burrow 1982); both are excellent up-to-date surveys.

Chapter 2   Aquae Sulis: The Roman Spa

The Roman period has been fairly extensively dealt with: for early accounts see Pownall 1795, Warner 1797, Scarth 1864, Haverfield 1906 and Knowles 1926. A summary of everything together with full references is to be found in Cunliffe 1969 which deals extensively with the baths. More recent excavations are reported in Cunliffe 1976, Cunliffe (ed.) 1979 and Cunliffe & Davenport 1985, the latter being a detailed report on the excavation of the Temple of Sulis Minerva. The most accessible summary of the temple and the baths is in the official guide book (Cunliffe 1985) which has a series of excellent illustrations.

Chapter 3   From Pagan to Christian: the Saxon rebirth

There is little written on the subject. For a summary of the period (with full references) see Cunliffe 1984b. The poem The Ruin is considered in Cunliffe 1983 with a commentary on the text and its relevance to recent archaeological discoveries. For the nature of the early monastery see Sims-Williams 1974. The Saxon mint is discussed in Grinsell 1973. Taylor 1900 gives a broad historical perspective of the period. The Saxon defences are considered in O'Leary 1981, while Grinsell 1974 gives a brief but fascinating insight into the Viking episode.

Chapter 4   Monks and wool: the medieval city

Ecclesiastical history has been extensively dealt with and fully referenced in Page 1911. The two major Chartularies with an extensive commentary are presented in Hunt 1893. The same author has also published a more general ecclesiastical history (Hunt 1885).

For the abbey itself see Britton 1825 and Brakspear n.d. Discoveries relating to the Norman cathedral priory are recorded by Irvine 1890 and Bond 1918.

The city walls have been considered on a number of occasions, in general by Lewis 1879 and in archaeological detail by Wedlake 1966 and O'Leary 1981.

The municipal records are fully treated in King & Watts n.d. and Shickle 1920 while the Poll Tax of Richard II is discussed by Green 1888.

For individual buildings: St. Werburga's (Greening 1966); St. James (Wedlake 1966); Abbey Church House (Boyd 1918); the Old Bridge (Green 1890); the two churches of St. Mary (King 1888); St. Michael's, Broad Street (McNeil 1936).

For a general history, not always reliable, consult Warner 1801.

Chapter 5   Dissolution and after: the sixteenth and seventeenth centuries

The most readable general account of the period emphasizing the history of the baths, is James 1938. Hamilton 1978 gives a summary of the urban topography of the city at the time. For the Civil War in Bath see Wroughton 1973.

There are numerous treatises extolling the virtues of the Bath waters especially Guidott 1676 and 1725 to which can be added Falconer 1772 and Oliver 1764 from a slightly later period.

Chapter 6   Elegance and expansion: the eighteenth century
There is no shortage of material. Excellent overviews of the period are given by
Melville 1926, Sitwell 1932 and Gadd 1971, and the architecture is most fully treated
in Green 1904 and Isons 1948. More anecdotal accounts of buildings can be found in
Meehan 1901 and 1906 and Peach 1883, 1884 and 1893. For specific buildings: the
Royal Crescent (Lowndes 1981), the Theatre Royal (Lowndes 1982), the Assembly
Rooms (National Trust 1979).
   The social and economic background has been thoroughly researched and
presented in McIntyre 1981 and Neal 1966 and 1981.
   Cultural and scientific life is considered in detail in Barbeau 1904 and Williams &
Stoddart 1978, other interesting works being Black 1926 and Williams 1946.
   There is also much excellent contemporary material such as the Bath guides, actual
and satirical, of Pope 1770 and Anstey 1767, but no-one should miss John Wood's
account of the city (Wood 1756).
   An invaluable catalogue of eighteenth and nineteenth century printed illustrations
is to be found in Lees-Milne and Ford 1982.

Chapter 7   The search for identity: 1800–1940
The social and economic development of the city in the early nineteenth century is
fully analyzed in Neal 1966 and 1981 and in Wroughton (ed.) 1972. Contemporary
chronicles such as Gibbes 1839 and Mainwaring 1838, are of particular interest.
   The revival of interest in the spa generated a spate of literature dealing with the
mineral springs including Anon 1901, Davis 1883, Fox 1890, Freeman 1888 and
Morris (ed.) 1888. There was also an outpouring of general books designed largely
for tourists including Davis 1864, Peach n.d., Tunstall 1889 and Wright 1864.
   Contemporary photographs and other material have been gathered in Ball 1972,
Croft 1982 and Hunt 1983, while Lees-Milne & Ford present a gallery of
contemporary prints.
   Some flavour of the dissension surrounding the fiery personality of Major Davis
can be gleaned from Anon 1884 and BSP 1894. For other personalities and civic
happenings see Murch 1893.

Chapter 8   Towards a future
The bombing of Bath in the Second World War is presented in Wainwright 1975
and Rothnie 1983.
   For the problems of post-war development Fergusson 1973 should not be missed.
The major planning documents are Buchanan et al. 1965 and 1968, Worskett et al.
1976 and 1978 and Anon 1980.

   If you have managed to read this far – a final word. Before you dive into the
literature suggested look at the city itself – it's worth it.

BIBLIOGRAPHY

IN THE FOLLOWING PAGES we offer a bibliography of Bath. It is by no means exhaustive. All the major, useful, works are here, and a lot more beside, but like most bibliographies it is biased towards the interests of its compiler and the text which it supports. Thus archaeology, topography and socio-economic history are well represented but political history, art and manners are rather more cursorily treated.

The more obscure books and papers have been omitted where they appear in the bibliographies of works cited. Three published bibliographies can be especially recommended to supplement what is offered here: in H.W. Freeman's *The Thermal Baths of Bath* (1888) there is a useful list of works relating to the mineral waters of Bath (pp. ix–xxiii); A. Barbeau, *Life and Letters at Bath in the XVIIIth Century* (1904) offers an impressive bibliography of works, generally of a more literary kind, referring to the city; and in *Images of Bath* by J. Lees-Milne and D. Ford a full listing is given of books containing illustrative material.

In addition to the printed works the Bath Reference Library possesses the voluminous manuscript notes of the meticulous local antiquary J.T. Irvine who was present in Bath, researching and recording in his spare time while working as Clerk of Works to Sir Gilbert Scott, between 1868 and 1872. The Irvine Manuscripts are of incomparable value to the local historian. Nor should we overlook the fine collection of manuscripts and drawings preserved in the Bath city archives. Rather disorganized forays in pursuance of particular themes have impressed upon the writer how much there is to be done. Finally the files of local newspapers kept by the Bath Reference Library are full of fascinating detail. The *Bath Journal* (1744–1916), the *Bath Advertiser* (later the *Bath Weekly Chronicle*) (began 1755), the *Bath Herald* (1792–1925) and the *Bath and Cheltenham Gazette* (1812–1897) are fully represented. Through their columns the personalities and issues come alive.

A. Books and Pamphlets Devoted to Bath

ANON 1884: *The pretended discovery of a Roman Bath at Bath* (Wyman & Son: London).

ANON 1901: *Medical Guide to the Hot Mineral Baths of Bath* (The Herald Office: Bath).

ANON 1980: *Policies for the Conservation Area* (Bath City Council: Bath).

ANSTEY, C. 1767 : *The New Bath Guide* (J. Dodsley: London).

ARMSTRONG, W. 1838: *An Account of the Tapping and Closing of a hot spring, Bath* (Wright: Bristol).

BALL, A. 1972: *Yesterday in Bath: A camera record 1849–1949* (Kingsmead Press: Bath).

BARBEAU, A. 1904: *Life and Letters at Bath in the XVIIIth Century* (Heinemann: London).

BLACK, C. 1926: *The Linleys of Bath* (Martin Secker: London).

BRAKSPEAR, H. n.d.: *Bath Abbey* (Brit. Pub. Co.: Gloucester).

BRITTON, J. 1825: *The history and antiquities of Bath Abbey Church* (Longman: London).

BSP 1894: *The Pump Room Competition, its history, rise and fall* (The Herald Office: Bath).

BUCHANAN, C. et al. 1965: *Bath: a Planning and Transport Study* (Buchanan & Partners: London).

BUCHANAN, C. et al. 1968: *Bath: a Study in Conservation* (HMSO: London).

CROFTS, B. 1982: *Forgotten Year. News from Bath in 1882* (Bath City Council: Bath).

CUNLIFFE, B. 1969: *Roman Bath* (Soc. of Antiq. Res. Report XXIV: London).

CUNLIFFE, B. 1971: *Roman Bath Discovered* (2nd edn. 1984) (Routledge & Kegan Paul: London).

CUNLIFFE, B. (ed.) 1979: *Excavations in Bath 1950–1975* (Cottee. Res. Arch. in Avon, Glos. & Som. Monograph 1: Bath).

CUNLIFFE, B. 1985: *The Roman Baths and Museum* (Bath Archaeological Trust: Bath).

CUNLIFFE, B. & DAVENPORT, P. 1985: *The Temple of Sulis Minerva at Bath. Volume 1 (I & II): The Site* (Oxford Univ. Cottee. for Archaeology Monograph no. 7: Oxford).

DAVIS, C.E. 1864: *Ancient Landmarks of Bath* (Wm. Lewis: Bath).

DAVIS, C.E. 1883: *The Mineral Bath of Bath. The Bathes of Bathe's Ayde in the reign of Charles 2nd* (Wm. Lewis & Son: Bath).

FALCONER, W. 1772: *An Essay on the Bath Waters* (Lowndes: London).

FERGUSSON, A. 1973: *The Sack of Bath: a record and an indictment* (Compton Russell: Salisbury).

FOX, A.E.W. 1890: *A Short Manual of the Bath Mineral Waters* (Simpkin, Marshall & Co.: London).

FREEMAN, H.W. 1888: *The Thermal Baths of Bath* (Hamilton, Adams & Co.: London).

GADD, D. 1971: *Georgian Summer* (Adams & Dart: Bath).

GIBBES, G.S. 1839: *The Bath Visitant*

GREEN, M.A. 1904: *The Eighteenth Century Architecture of Bath* (George Gregory: Bath).

GRINSELL, L.V. 1973: *The Bath Mint* (Spinks: London).

GUIDOTT, T. 1676: *A Discourse of Bath and the Hot waters there* (Brome: London).

GUIDOTT, T. 1725: *A Collection of Treatises relating to the City and Waters of Bath* (Leake: London).

HADDON, J. 1973: *Bath* (Batsford).

HAMILTON, M. 1978: *Bath Before Beau Nash* (Kingsmead Press: Bath).

HUNT, S. 1983: *A Bath Camera 1850–1950* (Dovecote Press: Wimborne).

HUNT, W. 1885: *The Somerset Diocese, Bath & Wells* (SPCK: London).

HUNT, W. 1893: *Two Chartularies of the Priory of St. Peter at Bath* (Somerset Record Society Vol. 7: London).

ISON, W. 1948: *The Georgian Buildings of Bath from 1700–1830* (Faber & Faber: London).

JAMES, P.R. 1938: *The Baths of Bath in the sixteenth and early seventeenth centuries* (Arrowsmith: Bristol).

KING, A.J. & WATTS, B.H. n.d.: *The Municipal Records of Bath 1189–1604* (Elliot Stock: London).

LEES-MILNE, J. & FORD, D. 1982: *Images of Bath* (St. Helena Press: Richmond-upon-Thames).

LITTLE, B. 1947: *The Building of Bath* (Collins: London).

LOWNDES, W. 1981: *The Royal Crescent in Bath* (Radcliffe: Bristol).

LOWNDES, W. 1982: *The Theatre Royal at Bath* (Radcliffe: Bristol).

MAINWARING, R. 1838: *The Annals of Bath, from the Year 1800 to the Passing of the New Municipal Act* (Meyler and Son: Bath).

McNEIL, H.C. 1936: *The Story of a Bath Parish. St. Michael's outside the North Gate* (Sharp: Bath).

MEEHAN, J.F. 1901: *Famous Houses of Bath & District* (Meehan: Bath).

MEEHAN, J.F. 1906: *More Famous Houses of Bath & District* (Meehan: Bath).

MEVILLE, L. 1926: *Bath under Beau Nash – and after* (Nash & Grayson: London).

MORRIS, J.W. (ed.) 1888: *Handbook to Bath prepared on the occasion of the visit of the British Association 1888* (Pitman & Sons: Bath).

MURCH, J. 1893: *Biographical Sketches of Bath Celebrities ancient and modern with some fragments of Local History* (Pitman & Sons: London).

NATIONAL TRUST 1979: *Bath Assembly Rooms* (National Trust: London).

NEAL, R.S. 1981: *Bath: A Social History 1680–1850* (Routledge & Kegan Paul: London).

OLIVER, W. 1764: *A practical dissertation on Bath-Waters* (Leake: London).

PEACH, R.E. n.d.: *Graphic Views in Bath and its Vicinity* (Peach: Bath).

PEACH, R.E. 1883: *Historic Houses in Bath and Their associations* (Simpkin, Marshall & Co.: London).

PEACH, R.E. 1884: *Historic Houses in Bath and Their associations II* (Simpkin, Marshall & Co.: London).

PEACH, R.E.M. 1893: *Street-Lore of Bath* (Simpkin, Marshall & Co.: London).

POPE, C. 1770 (and after): *The New Bath Guide or useful Pocket Companion* (Cruttwell: Bath).

POWNALL, T. 1795: *Descriptions and Explanations of Some remains of Roman Antiquities dug up in the City of Bath in the year MDCCXC* (Cruttwell: Bath).

ROBERTSON, C. 1975: *Bath: an Architectural Guide* (Faber & Faber: London).

ROTHNIE, N. 1983: *The Bombing of Bath* (Ashgrove Press: Bath).

SCARTH, H.M. 1864: *Aquae Solis or Notices of Roman Bath* (Simpkin, Marshall & Co.: London).

SHICKLE, C.W. 1920: *Ancient Deeds of the City of Bath XIII–XVIth Centuries* (Somerset Records Society: Bath).

SITWELL, E. 1932: *Bath* (Faber & Faber: London).

SMITH, R.A.L. 1944: *Bath* (Batsford: London).

SPENDER, C. & THOMPSON, E. 1922: *The Story of English Towns. Bath* (SPCK: London).

STONE, B.G. 1973: *Bath Millennium. The Christian Movement 973–1973* (Bath).

THOMSON, F.G. (President) 1925: *The Book of Bath* (written for the ninety-third Annual Meeting of the British Medical Association held in Bath in July 1925) (Bath).

TUNSTALL, J. 1889 (originally published 1847): *Rambles about Bath and its Neighbourhood* (based on Dr. Tunstall's work) (Pitman & Son: Bath).

WAINWRIGHT, M. 1975: *The Bath Blitz* (Kingston Press: Bath).

WARNER, R. 1797: *An Illustration of the Roman Antiquities Discovered at Bath* (Meyler: Bath).

WARNER, R. 1801: *The History of Bath* (Cruttwell: Bath).

WILLIAMS, M. 1946: *Lady Luxborough Goes to Bath* (Blackwells: Oxford).

WILLIAMS, W.J. & STODDART, D.M. 1978: *Bath – Some encounters with Science* (Kingsmead Press: Bath).

WOOD, J. 1765: *A Description of Bath*. Second edition, corrected and enlarged (Bathoe and Lownds: London).

WORSKETT, R. et al. 1976: *City of Bath Conservation Study: first stage report* (Bath City Council: Bath).

WORSKETT, R. et al. 1978: *Saving Bath: A programme for Conservation* (Conservation Study Stage 2 final Report) (Bath City Council: Bath).

WRIGHT, G.N. 1864: *The Historic Guide to Bath* (Peach: Bath).

WRISTON, B. 1978: *Rare Doings at Bath* (Art Inst. of Chicago: Chicago).

WROUGHTON, J. (ed.) 1972: *Bath in the Age of Reform (1830–1841)* (Morgan Books: Bath).

WROUGHTON, J. 1973: *The Civil War in Bath and North Somerset* (Bath).

B. Papers on Bath and the neighbourhood in books and journals

ANDREWS, J.N., BURGESS, W.G., EDMUNDS, W.M., KAY, R.L.F. and LEE, D.J. 1982: The thermal springs of Bath. *Nature* vol. 298 (22 July 1982), 339–43.

ASTON, M. & BURROW, I. (eds.) 1982: Chapter 7 in *The Archaeology of Somerset* (Taunton), 53–61.

BOND, F.B. 1918: Bath Abbey. Discovery of part of the Norman Triforium Arcade in the West Wall of the former Transept (south) now the east wall of the South Aisle of the Choir. *Proc. Bath Branch of the Somerset Archaeol. & Nat. Hist. Soc.* 3 (1914–18), 48–9.

BOYD, S.A. 1918: Abbey Church House. *Proc. Bath Branch of the Somerset Archaeol. & Nat. Hist. Soc.* 3 (1914–18), 224–7.

CUNLIFFE, B. 1976: The Roman Baths at Bath: Excavations 1969–75. *Britannia* VII, 1–32.

CUNLIFFE, B. 1983: Earth's Grip Holds Them. In Hartley, B. and Wacher, J. (eds.), *Rome and her Northern Provinces* (Sutton: Gloucester), 67–83.

CUNLIFFE, B. 1984a: Gloucestershire and the Iron Age of Southern Britain. *Trans. Bristol & Glos. Archaeol. Soc.* 102, 5–15.

CUNLIFFE, B. 1984b: Saxon Bath. In Haslam, J. (ed.), *Anglo-Saxon Towns in Southern England* (Phillimore: Chichester), 345–358.

DOWDEN, W.A. 1957: Little Solsbury Hill Camp. *Proc. Univ. Bristol Spelaeol. Soc.* 8(1), 18–29.

DOWDEN, W.A. 1962: Little Solsbury Hill Camp. *Proc. Univ. Bristol Spelaeol. Soc.* 9(3), 177–82.

GREEN, E. 1888: A Bath Poll Tax 2 Richard II. *Proc. Bath. Nat. Hist. & Antiq. field Club* VI(3), 294–315.

GREEN, E. 1890: Bath Old Bridge, and the Oratory thereon. *Proc. Bath Nat. Hist. & Antiq. field Club* VII(1), 25–34.

GREENING, P.J. 1966: St. Werburga's by Bath. *A North Somerset Miscellany* (Bath), 20–24.

GRIMES, W.F. 1960: *Excavations on Defence Sites 1939–1954* (HMSO: London), Chapter VIII: The Archaeology of Charmy Down, near Bath, Somerset, 99–244.

GRINSELL, L.V. 1974: A Viking burial in a stone coffin in Bath. *Somerset & Dorset Notes and Queries* 30, 67.

HAVERFIELD, F. 1906: Bath. In Page, W. (ed.), *The Victoria County History of the County of Somerset* Vol. 1 (Street: London), 219–288.

IRVINE, J.T. 1890: Description of the Remains of the Norman Cathedral of Bath exposed during the repairs made between 1863 and 1872. *Journal of the British Archaeol. Ass.*, 85–94.

KELLAWAY, G.A. 1985: The Geomorphology of the Bath region. In Cunliffe B. and Davenport, P., *The Temple of Sulis Minerva at Bath. Volume 1 (I & II): The Site* (Oxford Univ. Cottee. for Archaeology Monograph no. 7: Oxford), 4–8.

KING, A.J. 1888: The Destruction of the two Churches of St. Mary in Bath. *Proc. Bath Nat. Hist. & Antiq. field Club* VI(3), 285–94.

KNOWLES, W.H. 1926: The Roman Baths at Bath; with an Account of the excavations conducted during 1923. *Archaeologia* LXXV, 1–18.

LEWIS, H. 1879: The Old Walls of the City of Bath. *Proc. Bath Nat. Hist. & Antiq. field Club* IV(2), 138–49.

McINTYRE, S. 1981: Bath: The rise of a resort town, 1660–1800. In Clark, P. (ed.), *Country Towns in pre-industrial England* (University Press: Leicester), 198–249.

NEAL, R.S. 1966: The Standard of Living 1780–1844: a Regional Class Study. *Economic History Review* XIX,.

O'LEARY, T. 1981: Excavations at Upper Borough Wall, Bath, 1980. *Medieval Archaeol.* 25, 1–30.

PAGE, W. (ed.) 1911: Benedictine Houses: 1 The Cathedral Priory of Bath. In *Victoria County History of Somerset Vol. II* (Oxford), 69–81.

SAVILLE, A. (ed.) 1984: Chapter in *Archaeology in Gloucestershire* (Cheltenham), 140–78.

SIMS-WILLIAMS, P. 1974: Continental influence at Bath monastery in the seventh century. *Anglo-Saxon England* 4, 1–10.

TAYLOR, C.S. 1900: Bath, Mercian and West Saxon. *Trans. Bristol & Glos. Archaeol. Soc.* 23, 129–61.

TRATMAN, E.K. 1973: flint implements from the Bath Downs. *Proc. Univ. Bristol Spelaeol. Soc.* 13(2), 153–69.

WAINWRIGHT, G.J. 1967: The Excavation of an Iron Age Hillfort on Bathampton Down, Somerset. *Trans. Bristol & Glos. Archaeol. Soc.* 86, 42–59.

WAINWRIGHT, G.J. 1970: An Iron Age Promontory Fort at Budbury, Bradford-on-Avon, Wiltshire. *Wilts. Archaeol. Mag.* 65, 108–166.

WEDLAKE, W.J. 1966: The city walls of Bath, the church of St. James, South Gate and the area to the east of the church of St. James. *Proc. Somerset Archaeol. & Nat. Hist. Soc.* 110, 85–107.

WILLIAMS, A. 1950: Bronze Age Barrows on Charmy Down and Lansdown, Somerset. *Antiquaries Journal* 30, 34–46.

INDEX

Figures in bold are illustration numbers. Other references are to pages